How to be Entertaining

Also by Andrew Wright

In this series:
How to Communicate Successfully
How to Enjoy Paintings
How to Improve Your Mind
How to be a Successful Traveller

with David Betteridge and Michael Buckby:
Games for Language Learning

How to be Entertaining

Andrew Wright

with drawings by the author

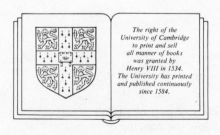

The right of the
University of Cambridge
to print and sell
all manner of books
was granted by
Henry VIII in 1534.
The University has printed
and published continuously
since 1584.

Cambridge University Press
Cambridge
London   New York   New Rochelle
Melbourne   Sydney

Published by the Press Syndicate of the University of Cambridge
The Pitt Building, Trumpington Street, Cambridge CB2 1RP
32 East 57th Street, New York, NY 10022, USA
10 Stamford Road, Oakleigh, Melbourne 3166, Australia

© Cambridge University Press 1986

First published 1986

Printed in Great Britain
at the Bath Press, Avon

ISBN 0 521 27549 0

SE

Contents

Contents

Thanks

I would like to thank Alison Silver, the editor of this series who has made a significant contribution to each book in terms of content and presentation. I would also like to thank Monica Vincent for her valuable advice, Peter Donovan for his support during the long period of writing and Peter Ducker for his concern for the design and typography. I am also grateful to the teachers and students of Nord Anglia for trying out samples of the texts and giving me useful advice for their improvement.

In a book of this kind one is naturally influenced by a large number of writers, lecturers, friends and acquaintances. However, I should like to acknowledge the following writers and their books in particular: J.M. and M.J. Cohen, *Modern Quotations*, Penguin; *The Oxford Dictionary of Quotations*, Oxford University Press; *The International Thesaurus of Quotations*, Penguin; Reg Bolton, *Circus in a Suitcase*, New Plays Inc.; Ralph Steadman, *Sigmund Freud*, Paddington Press; Robert Baldwin and Ruth Paris, *The Book of Similes*, Routledge Kegan Paul; Derek and Julia Parker, *How do you know who you are?*, Macmillan Publishing Co., New York; John Morgan and Mario Rinvolucri, *Once Upon A Time*, Cambridge University Press; Roald Dahl, *Kiss Kiss*, Penguin; Ann Petrie, *Everything You Ever Wanted to Know About Astrology But Thought You Shouldn't Ask*, Methuen; Jo Sheridan, *Teacup Fortune Telling*, Granada; Tom Chetwynd, *Dictionary for Dreamers*, Paladin; G. A. Dudley, *Dreams, Their Mysteries Revealed*, Aquarian Press; Lady Penelope, *Etiquette Today*, Paperfronts; Elsie Burch Donald (ed.), *Debrett's Etiquette and Modern Manners*, Pan; Rudi McToots, *The Kids' Book of Games for Cars, Trains and Planes*, Bantam Books Inc.; Richard Fisher, *Brain Games*, Fontana; Marjorie Palmer, *Adult Games*, Dell Publishing Co., New York.

About this book

How to be Entertaining is one in a series of five books. There are seven chapters, each dealing with a different aspect of being entertaining. There are several different sections in each chapter, and some will probably be more interesting and relevant to you than others. There is no need to read every section. I hope you will find it all interesting and that your reading of English will improve as well as your entertaining.

★ Indicates that there is a question you should think about on your own.
★★ Indicates that if you are reading the book with another person you should talk about this particular question with him or her.

You may be reading the book while studying English in a class, with a teacher, or you may be reading it at home in the evenings, or on a train, or anywhere else – it doesn't matter.

What I do hope is that you enjoy reading about being entertaining – in English!

Some thoughts on being entertaining

★ Do you agree with any of them?

Laugh, and the world laughs with you;
Weep, and you weep alone.

(Ella Wheeler Wilcox, 'Solitude', *Collected Poems*, 1917)

There is nothing in which people more betray their character than in what they laugh at.

(Goethe, *Elective Affinities*, 1809)

All that the comedian has to show for his years of work and aggravation is the echo of forgotten laughter.

(Fred Allen, *Treadmill to Oblivion*, 1954)

Everything is funny as long as it is happening to somebody else.

(Will Rogers, 'Warning to Jokers: Lay Off the Prince,' *The Illiterate Digest*, 1942)

The most wasted day is that in which we have not laughed.

(Chamfort, *Maximes et Pensées*, 1805)

One can know a man from his laugh, and if you like a man's laugh before you know anything of him, you may confidently say that he is a good man.

(Dostoyevsky, *The House of the Dead*, 1862)

You are not angry with people when you laugh at them. Humour teaches tolerance.

(W. Somerset Maugham, *The Summing Up*, 1938)

Humour is the first of the gifts to perish in a foreign tongue.

(Virginia Woolf, 'On Not Knowing Greek,' *The Common Reader: First Series*, 1925)

The secret of being a bore is to tell everything.

(Voltaire, *Sept discours en vers sur l'homme*, 1738)

Bore, noun. A person who talks when you wish him to listen.

(Ambrose Bierce, *The Devil's Dictionary*, 1881–1911)

A healthy male adult bore consumes each year one and a half times his own weight in other people's patience.

(John Updike, 'Confessions of a Wild Bore,' *Assorted Prose*, 1965)

A bore is a man who, when you ask him how he is, tells you.

(Bert Leston Taylor, quoted in A. Andrews, *Quotations for Speakers and Writers*)

It is only the very young girl at her first dinner-party whom it is difficult to entertain. At her second dinner-party, and thereafter, she knows the whole art of being amusing. All she has to do is to listen; all we men have to do is to tell her about ourselves.

(A.A. Milne (1882–1956), *Going Out to Dinner*)

To get into society nowadays, one has either to feed people, amuse people, or shock people.

(Oscar Wilde, *A Woman of No Importance*, 1893)

There is pleasure in hardship heard about.

(Euripides, *Helen*, 412 BC)

An honest tale speeds best being plainly told.

(Shakespeare, *Richard III*, 1592–93)

There are several kinds of stories, but only one difficult kind – the humorous.

(Mark Twain, *How to Tell a Story*, 1895)

'The story is like the wind,' the Bushman prisoner said. 'It comes from a far off place, and we feel it.'

(Laurens Van Der Post (b.1906), *A Story Like the Wind*)

It is a happy talent to know how to play.

(Emerson, *Journals*, 1834)

There are toys for all ages.

(English Proverb)

In our play we reveal what kind of people we are.

(Ovid, *The Art of Love*, c. 8 AD)

There is a time and a place for everything

(English Proverb)

It takes all sorts to make a world.

(English Proverb)

Andrew Wright juggling with silk scarves.

Your pleasure is mine

The success of the ideas in this book depends on several things: your personality, the personality of the other person (or people), the occasion and the place where you are.

You

I very much hope you will find some interesting and useful ideas in this book. But I am sure you will agree with me that no one can learn these ideas and simply become entertaining! Some people are naturally quiet and enjoy listening and encouraging other people to speak. And that is one way of being entertaining. Most of the activities in this book can be done quietly!

Other sorts of people don't mind talking to a lot of people; they may even want to control everything and organise all the entertainment! And such people can be a wonderful asset to a party.

★ What do you enjoy doing?

The other person or people

What does the other person (or do the other people) want and expect? That is a more useful question than asking how old they are or whether they are men, women or children. For example, some old people are full of youthful fun and some young people are rather old-fashioned. So people's personalities are more important than their age.

The relationship between you and the other person or people is important. Are you and the other people strangers? Do you know each other very well or only a little? If you don't know them how can you entertain them? What sort of entertainment is 'safe'? Usually the best way to entertain a stranger is to listen to them and make them feel that you are interested in them. In this way you give pleasure and, at the same time, you learn about them so that you will know how to be entertaining in other ways.

The occasion

Some people tell jokes and stories and make people laugh or be deeply moved. Other people try to tell a story or a joke which may be just as good but . . . total failure! Laughter, emotion, and the wish to understand are all within each person. The successful entertainer releases laughter, emotion and interest, but he or she can't put them there. There are moments when people are ready to be interested and ready to laugh and there are moments when they aren't.

A good entertainer is very sensitive to the right and wrong moment. The good entertainer listens and looks to see how the other person is feeling. Of course, a good entertainer can create the right mood and expectation before beginning their story, game or magic trick, and will find a way of linking what they want to do with what has been happening.

This book

Please don't try to read this book from cover to cover! Begin with any part of any section and try it out. But do try the ideas, please don't just read about them. When you try them you will find your own way of doing them, according to your personality and that of your friends. If you are a quiet sort of person you can still do all of these ideas: they don't need a large audience. Almost all the activities in this book can be done with one or two people only.

The last chapter of the book is intended for those of you who are going to visit an English speaking country. It gives advice on how to be entertained when you are in Britain. It is an art to be entertained! You must understand your hosts and then you and they can share a good time together.

How to astonish your friends

Magic tricks

If you like, you can do tricks at a party and be announced as, 'The Magician'. However, the best time to entertain people with tricks is when they aren't expecting it. I am sure you know those times when you go out with your friends for the evening, perhaps to a pub or a restaurant, when everybody wants a bit of fun but nothing really happens. That is the moment to start one of these tricks. You won't need any special materials for these tricks, nor will you need to practise them very much!

Tricks with coins

A COIN AND TWO SAUCERS

Turn the saucers upside down. Put the coin beneath one of the saucers. Say to your friends, 'I am going to make the coin go from beneath that saucer to beneath that saucer.' Hold out your hands and make them shake as if magic is coming out of them. Point them at the saucer with the coin beneath it.

Then move your hands across to the other saucer.

Look under the other saucer and show astonishment that the coin is not there! Look under the first saucer and see the coin. Frown! Do the magic again. And once more, find that the coin hasn't moved. Do the magic again. But this time, when you pick up the second saucer to see if the coin has arrived don't let other people see!

Show relief and triumph as if it has arrived and then say, with triumph, 'Yes!' and add with great seriousness, 'Now, ladies and gentlemen, for the first time in . . . I am going to make it go back again!'

Rapidly do your magic action as everyone laughs and then lift the first saucer and find the coin. Hold it up and shout, 'I've done it!'

A COIN AND A PIECE OF PAPER

Put the coin under the piece of paper and say, 'I am going to pick up the coin but I am not going to pick up the piece of paper!'

Point all your fingers at the paper and say, 'Kaboom!' Then ask someone to help you. Say to them, 'Have a look!' And point at the paper. They will probably pick up the paper or at least, raise it a little. Pick up the coin, and say, 'I picked up the coin but I didn't pick up the paper!'

This makes the other person look a bit foolish . . . and they only did it to help you, so give them an apology!

A POUND NOTE (or any other currency note) a pile of coins and a glass of beer (or any other liquid!)

Put the pound note on the rim of the glass. Put the pile of coins on the pound note. Ask your friend to remove the pound note but not to touch the coins. It's difficult! The answer is to pull the note very quickly! You can also try this trick with a table cloth but get ready to leave quickly if one of your friends smashes all the plates, etc.

A COIN

Say to one of your friends, 'I am going to put this coin where everybody can see it except you!' Put it on his or her head.

A COIN, A HANDKERCHIEF AND A FRIEND

Put the coin on your palm. Cover the coin with the handkerchief. Ask several people to put their hand beneath the handkerchief and feel the coin, to make sure that it is still there. Then take the corner of the handkerchief and pull it rapidly off your hand. The coin has gone! How? You must make sure the last friend knows the trick! Your last

friend removes the coin when he or she seems to be just feeling it. And nobody knows where it has gone!

FIVE COINS

Ask your friends if they think they are clever. Put out five coins like this:

Say, 'You have got three moves. Each time you must move two touching coins. And you must finish with the three 10p coins at the beginning of the row and the two 5p coins at the end of the row.'

It is difficult! The answer is to:
- move coin C and coin D to the right of coin E;
- move coin E and coin C to the space where C and D were;
- move A and B to the empty space where E and C were.

Tricks with matches

ELEVEN MATCHES

Put ten matches on the table. Count them out. Take one more match from your box. Give it to your friend and say, 'Here's one more match. Now see if you can make nine! And you mustn't take any away.'
Here is the answer!

NINE

TWENTY FOUR MATCHES

Arrange them like this.

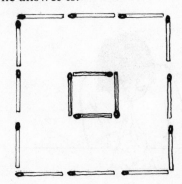

Now tell your friend to take away eight matches and to leave only two squares. The answer is:

5

A MATCH BOX

Take the drawer out of the box and put it like this:

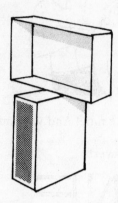

Ask your friend if he or she is strong. 'Do you think you can break that match box? Try to break it with your fist.'

It will be impossible because it will always fall down.

TWO MATCHES

Put the two matches on the table about 10cm apart. Say you have a strange power in your finger. 'Watch this. I can make the matches move apart without touching them!'

As you place your finger down in between the matches keep your head above them and blow gently downwards. The matches will move apart!

SOME MATCHES

One match for each of your friends. For a few seconds before your trick make the wooden end of your match wet. Then stand it on the table. Challenge everyone else to do the same. Give them each a match. Their matches will fall down!

A BOX OF MATCHES

You must prepare this trick before you meet your friends. Get a half-full box of matches. Take one match and break it so that you have a length which is equal to the width of your box. Put it across the top of the other matches so that it is fixed and stops the other matches from moving.

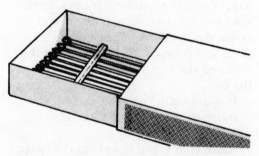

Show your friends the box and say that the matches will only fall out of the box when you tell them to! Hold the box upside down. The matches don't fall out. Then tell the matches to fall out and they do! Why?

As you speak to the matches you must close the box and hold it at each end of the drawer. Squeeze the drawer and this will release the short match which is fixed inside. Then they will all fall out!

Tricks with drinks

TWO GLASSES, WATER AND A COIN

Say that you are going to balance one glass upside down and full of water on top of the other.

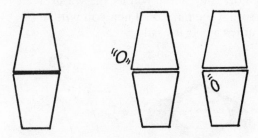

After your friends have expressed their amazement and disbelief put both glasses under water and fill them. Join the open ends together and take them out of the water. Stand them on the table. Wait for the applause.

Now, say that you are going to put a coin inside the lower glass. Tap the upper glass with a knife or the coin, gently. After a moment the glass will lift very slightly. Push your coin carefully through the gap between the two glasses. Wait for the applause.

Now say that you are going to take out all the water from the top glass without touching it! Position one friend on the other side of the glass and then blow hard at the gap between the two glasses. The water will come out and he or she will be sprayed with it.

THREE GLASSES OR CUPS

They must be identical. Put them like this:

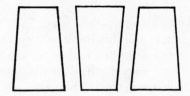

Make two moves:
– turn the first two over
– turn the second two over
And the glasses will finish the right way up.

Do this several times and then ask your friends to do it. But put the glasses like this for them:

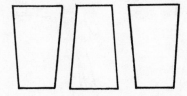

Tell them they have two moves to get all the glasses the right way up. And they won't be able to do it.

A GLASS OF BEER

You could do this with water but it really is best to do it in a pub or at a party with a glass of beer or a glass of wine!

When you have everyone's attention, put your pint on the table and say loudly and boastfully, 'Do you think I can leave my pint here, go out of the pub and, without walking back in, drink it up?' All your friends will shout, 'No!' and wait to see what you are going to do!

Go out of the pub, *crawl* back in, up to the table, and drink up the beer!

Tricks with . . . all sorts of things

A BOOK I

Hold a book against the wall. Say, 'I am going to tell this book to stay against the wall! Book, stay against the wall! Don't move! Oh, wait a minute, I need something else!' Then ask someone to come and hold the book for you. They come and hold the book and you stand back and say, 'There you are, I told you I could make the book stay against the wall without my holding it!'

A PIECE OF PAPER AND A PENCIL

Say that you can communicate your thoughts to people. Write on the piece of paper the word, No. Don't let your friends see what you have written. Say, 'Now I will communicate this word into your minds.' Pretend to concentrate. Ask someone if he or she knows what is written on the piece of paper. They will say, 'No!' And you say, 'Quite correct! I wrote on the paper, No!'

A NAPKIN

Ask if anyone can tear a paper napkin in half. Twist the napkin into a rope and give it to the strongest person. He or she won't be able to tear it! Make sure your fingers are wet and take the napkin from him or her. Talk for a short time while you let the water soften the napkin. Then you will be able to tear it easily.

A PIECE OF STRING

Ask your friend if he or she can hold a piece of string at each end and tie a knot in it without letting go.

This is how to do it. First of all, fold your arms and then get hold of the string. Then unfold your arms!

TWO BROOM HANDLES AND A LONG PIECE OF STRING

Ask who are the two strongest people amongst your friends. Then ask for the weakest friend. Say that you are going to show everyone that it isn't true. 'You are all quite wrong. You don't know how strong . . . really is!'

Tell each of the strong friends to hold a broom handle vertically. Tell

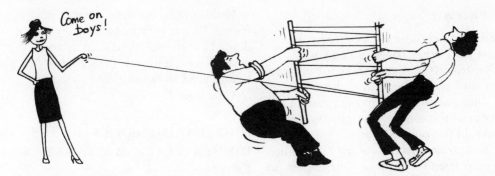

them that they mustn't let it move! Tie one end of the string to the top of one of the brooms. Take the string across to the other broom, around it and back again. Go to and fro until the string is as it is in the picture.

Then tell the weak friend to pull! He or she should be able to pull so that both broom handles come together!

TWO LUMPS OF SUGAR

Say that your eyes glow in the dark. Turn off the lights. Rub the two lumps of sugar together and then hold them in front of your eyes. They will make a strange glow!

AN EGG AND SOME SALT

Ask your friends to stand the egg upright on the table. They won't manage to do it. Say that you can speak to the chicken inside. Say, 'Chicken! Can you hear me? Get ready to balance your egg!'

When you first get the egg back from your friends pretend to kiss the egg at the base. Make the base wet. Then put the base into salt which is in your other hand. The salt will stick to the egg. Then put the egg on the table. Twist

the egg around a few times as this will arrange the grains of salt. Then it will stand up. Don't forget to thank the chicken.

TWO IDENTICAL BOOKS: TELEPATHY

Before you see your friends, hide one of the books behind a curtain or outside the room, etc. Say, 'I can read the words in your mind.' Give someone the book. Say that you will go out of the room or behind the curtain. 'When I am out of the room/behind the curtain, open the book and find a line on the page. Tell me which page and line it is and I will tell you what the words are.'

You simply look up the page and the line in the copy of the book. And, with a little hesitation and perhaps one or two mistakes, call out the words!

A FRIEND

Tell one friend the trick before you meet your other friends. Tell your other friends that you and your partner can read each other's thoughts.

Your partner stays in the room. You go out of the room. A number is chosen and told to your partner.

You come into the room. You go up to your friend and place your fingers on his or her temples. Your friend must then tighten his or her jaw for each number. When he or she does this you will feel the temples move and you can count the number of times he or she does it. Your friend must wait for a second or two between each number.

A SCARF OR A PIECE OF CLOTH AND A FRIEND

Cut a hole in a piece of cloth beforehand. Tell your friends that you and your partner can communicate telepathically. Your friend must stand sideways on to all the other friends. Tie the cloth around his or her eyes and make sure that the hole is over the eye away from your friends!

Hold up objects in front of your friend. 'What is this object? Can you describe it to me?' And your friend describes each object. (Tell him or her beforehand to hesitate and to make a few mistakes!)

NINE CARDS, BOOKS OR DINNER PLACE MATS, AND A FRIEND

This is a wonderfully successful and easy trick! It is done in two stages: the first is the easy stage and the second the difficult one. But it is easy and difficult for your friends and not for you!

You must teach the two parts of the trick to your 'assistant' beforehand.

Part one
Put nine books, etc. in a pattern like this:

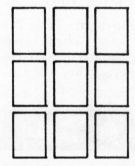

Then ask if anyone believes in telepathy. Get an argument going! Say you are going to prove that telepathy can work. Ask your assistant to go out of the room. The other people decide which one of the books they are all going to think about and they tell you.

Your assistant comes back into the room. You point at a book and say, 'Is it this one?' He or she says, 'No.' And then you continue until you point to the one chosen and he or she says, 'Yes.'

Your assistant knows which one it is by the way you point at the first book. The nine books are arranged in a rectangle. If the other people have chosen, for example, the top left-hand corner book you must point to the top left-hand corner of the first book you point to! If they choose the middle book then you must point to the middle of the first book you point to. In other words your assistant knows after the first book you point to.

Some people will realise what you are doing very quickly. If there are some rather clever people there, move on to part two!

Part two
If they say you are signalling to your assistant then pretend to be rather hurt and astonished by their suspicions. Say that before your assistant comes back into the room you will hide so that he or she can't see you.

Of course you must leave your signal! It could be left on another book, a piece of paper or a place mat, etc. When you go to hide you must leave something on the piece of paper in the right position. You might, for example, leave a glass of wine or a little ball of paper on the piece of paper.

Your assistant then comes back into the room, sees the little ball of paper on the piece of paper, notices the position

and then knows which one has been chosen (in the drawing it is the middle book on the right).

It takes time to describe to you but it is really very easy to do. And the effect is amazing!

FLOUR, CIGARETTE ASH OR POWDER

A few minutes before you do this trick, put some of the flour, ash or powder on one of your fingers. Don't let anyone see you doing this! Then during a drop in the conversation reach over the table and take hold of each of a friend's hands with each of yours. As you do so press the flour onto one of their palms, and make them tighten their hands into fists and turn them over so that the fingers are towards the floor.

Then put your finger into some more of the flour and wipe it onto the back of their other hand: the one which is clean on the palm! Now say, 'I am going to make this flour go up your arm, across your body and down your other arm and into your hand.' Then smack the hand with the flour, etc. on the outside, so that it disappears. Then make magic movements and direct the flour, etc. up the arm and across the

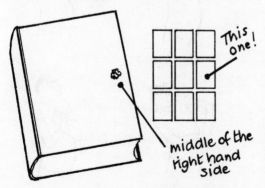

This one!

middle of the right hand side

body and down the other arm into the hand. 'Open your hand!' And to their astonishment the flour is in that hand!

YOUR FINGERS

Stand up. Raise your arms. Bend them so that your forearms are in front of your body. Touch the tips of your forefingers. Now, challenge anybody to try to pull your arms apart.

YOUR HEAD

Sit down. Put your hand on your head. Challenge anybody to pull your hand away from your head.

A BOOK 2

Practise with a book you don't want to keep! Put it on a table so that half of it projects over the edge. Hit the book on the underside with the back of your hand. The book will do a somersault

and you then catch it in the same hand. In Britain we have beer mats made out of stiff card and about 10cm across. Some people can make a pile of ten of them and catch them all in the air!

A WILLING FRIEND

Say to your friend, 'Can you wag the little finger of your left hand?' They will say, 'Yes,' and they will start to wag it. Tell them to stretch their arms straight out in front of them with the palms of their hands turned outwards. Tell them to cross their right arm over their left arm and to intertwine their fingers very tightly.

Now tell them to lower their arms to their body and then to bend them with the elbows forward . . . until the hands come up the chest and in front of the chin. Now tell them to wag the little finger of their left hand!

A PIECE OF PAPER

Look at your friend's hand in horror! Say, 'Look at that hole in your hand! What have you done to it? Can't you see it? I know it's only small but I can see right through it! Here let me give you my telescope and you will be able to see through it as well.'

Now, roll the paper so that the diameter is about 2cm. Then tell your friend to put it to their left eye. Then tell him or her to hold up his or her right hand, palm towards the face, next to the tube and about halfway down it. He or she must keep both eyes open. They should be able to see right through the middle of their hand!

A JACKET AND A FRIEND

Your friend must be male and wear a shirt, tie and jacket. Talk to your partner before you meet all your other friends. Tell him to take his jacket and his shirt off.

He must then put his shirt on like this:

SHIRT OVER SHOULDERS
FASTEN FIRST TWO BUTTONS
ARMS DO NOT GO INSIDE THE SLEEVES. DO UP THE CUFFS AT THE BOTTOM.

And then he must put his jacket back on. At some point in the evening tell your friend that you don't like his shirt! 'What do you want me to do?' says your friend, 'I can't take it off!' You say, 'If I can take it off for you without taking your jacket off will you let me throw it away?' You then undo his shirt cuff buttons. You take his tie off and undo the buttons at the top of his shirt. Then you take the shirt by the collar at the back and, with one sharp pull, out comes the shirt!

SOME TRICKS YOU CAN BUY

Circus tricks

Sophie is six, she is the youngest and smallest member of the family and so she loves walking on stilts! On stilts she is much taller than her brother Joe. Joe is only ten but he has performed in many countries with his family, from the United States to Japan. He is a talented unicyclist and juggler. Annie – in her own professional life she is a 'serious' mime artist – acts as a clown when playing with her family. Reg can ride a unicycle, juggle, eat fire, walk on a tight rope and do acrobatics. He has taught me most of the circus tricks I know.

above: *Joe, Sophie and Reg Bolton – 'The Suitcase Circus'.*

left: *Annie – the mime artist.*

below: *Unicycling. Tom Wright, Reg Bolton, Andrew Wright.*

Juggling

Reg taught me how to juggle, and I have juggled at parties, in schools and youth clubs and at street fairs. I once juggled with three wine glasses at a party on the twenty sixth floor of a hotel in Honolulu. All was going well, the glasses were flying beautifully when I lost my concentration. Outside the window I saw the moon break out from the clouds and spill flickering light across the Pacific Ocean. The glasses met in mid air and smashed. Little bits flew in all directions. I felt awful.

But as long as you concentrate all the time, most people can learn how to juggle. It usually takes about an hour to get the idea. Once you have learned to juggle you never forget. The best object to use when learning is a bean bag: bean bags don't roll away when you drop them.

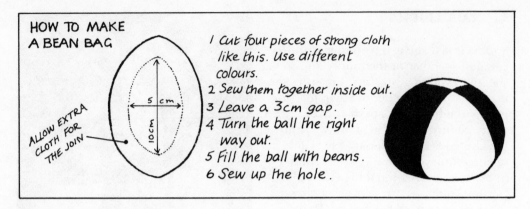

HOW TO MAKE A BEAN BAG

ALLOW EXTRA CLOTH FOR THE JOIN

5 cm

10 cm

1 Cut four pieces of strong cloth like this. Use different colours.
2 Sew them together inside out.
3 Leave a 3cm gap.
4 Turn the ball the right way out.
5 Fill the ball with beans.
6 Sew up the hole.

However, if you don't want to make bean bags, get three balls the size of tennis balls. It is better if they are heavier than tennis balls as tennis balls seem to hit the hand and then bounce out again.

Reg taught me the three ball cascade technique first, and this is what you do.

With one ball

First
Stand comfortably. Bend your arms so that your forearms are horizontal.

Keep your elbows next to your body (and keep them there when you are throwing as well!). Open your hands;

your palms should face upwards. Hold one ball in one hand.

Second
Throw the ball upwards and across so that it lands in your other hand. The ball should go as high as your forehead before descending. You should not move your other hand in order to catch the ball.

Third
Do this several times with each hand until you can do it without moving your catching hand and without moving your elbows.

With two balls

First
Stand as before. Hold a ball in each hand.

Second
Throw the first ball up and across as before. When the first ball is as high as your forehead throw the other ball up and across.

Problem?
You may not be waiting until the first ball is as high as your forehead. You may be trying to pass the second one across to the other hand. Children in most countries of the world seem to

juggle this way! And older people find it difficult to forget what they learned as a child.

Practice
Practise until you can keep your elbows still and by your sides; and until the balls land comfortably on to each hand.

Three balls

First
Stand as before. Hold two balls in one hand and one in the other.

Second
Throw one of the balls from the hand with two balls in it. When this ball is as high as your forehead, throw the ball from your other hand. When the second is as high as your forehead, throw the third one.

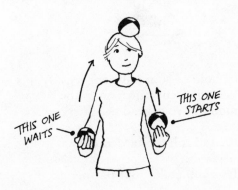

Practice
It is more important to get into the rhythm and to keep your elbows in against your sides than it is to catch the balls!

A WAY OF MAKING FRIENDS

Reg says,

'Some people juggle to impress people, others to relate to cosmic vibrations, others to make friends and share experiences. When I was in San Francisco, I heard that Saturday mornings were jugglers' gatherings at Golden Gate Park. As I wandered through the park, I approached the crest of a small hill. Ahead of me, the horizon was filled with balls, rings and clubs, buzzing about, intermingling like flies over a pond. Walking on a bit further, I saw the people – a layer of people beneath the layer of flying things. There were about sixty of them, young and old; black, brown and white; rich and poor. I was immediately made welcome, offered the loan of a set of balls, and began to learn and teach, and make friends.'

If you want to learn how to juggle with more balls and with a partner then you'd better get a copy of Reg's book, *Circus in a suitcase*! And there are lots of other ideas in it, like unicycling.

How to be an acrobat

Here are some ideas which look impressive but aren't too difficult to do.

ACROBATICS ON YOUR OWN

Headstand

First of all make sure that the ground is clear behind you. You might fall over! If you aren't confident ask someone to stand to one side of you and tell them to help you up. They mustn't stand behind you because you might kick them! You could, of course, do your first headstands against a wall.

Now find a nice, soft place for your head. You may need a folded blanket. Put the top of your head on the ground and then put your forearms on the ground and clasp your hands behind your head. Now make your back as straight as you can. The straighter you can make your back the easier it will be for you to raise your legs.

Begin to walk your feet towards your face. Keep your back straight. When you can't walk your legs any further lift them. It is easier if you bend them at this point. Raise them very slowly. Once you can balance you can:
– open your legs and turn them round
– pedal your legs as if you are on a bicycle
– cross your legs into the lotus position

Instead of clasping your hands behind your back you can place them just in front and to the side of your face, so your head and your two hands make a triangle.

ACROBATICS WITH A FRIEND

Tank roll

1 One of you must begin by standing, and the other by lying.
2 You must slowly bend forward.

Keep hold of your partner's legs. As his or her legs come down on to the ground put your head between them . . .
3 . . . and roll forward and do a somersault.
4 This will make your partner sit

upright. Then he or she can easily stand.

5 And your partner can start the process again.

After a little practice you will be able to do this at a great speed!

Spider!

You and your partner need to be very supple and able to bend very easily.

1 If you are the supple one . . . Put your hands behind your friend's neck and clasp them very firmly.

2 Jump up with your legs and clasp them round your friend's waist.

3 Keep hold with your legs and slowly let your body fall backwards until your hands can reach the ground.

4 Walk your hands forwards so that your body goes between your friend's legs.

5 Your friend must now bend forward and place his or her hands on the ground.

Now you have six legs and you can walk forwards or backwards – towards anyone who is frightened of spiders!

strong person

light person!

Shoulder stand

This technique depends on rhythm more than strength. Nevertheless, it is easier if one of you is quite strong and the other quite light.

1 Are you the strong one? Stand with your feet well apart. Bend your knees until your thighs are nearly horizontal.

2 Your friend must put her or his left foot on your left thigh. The foot must point inwards.

3 They must hold both of your hands. Their right hand must hold your right hand and their left your left. The right hands must be above the left hands.

4 Your friend must now swing his or her right foot up behind your back and onto your right shoulder. You must help by pulling upwards with your hands.

5 Then your friend can put his or her left foot on your left shoulder.

This is very useful for helping small people see over the heads of crowds. They can get down by jumping down in front of you, or they can sit down on your neck.

Eagle

Start with your partner sitting on your shoulders. Bend your legs until your thighs are nearly horizontal. Your partner now stands on your thighs. Bend your head and bring it backwards and through your partner's legs. He or she is now standing like an eagle!

How to tell jokes

Jokes and amusing remarks

What is it that makes people laugh? Freud, the psychologist, said, 'It is a fact that if we try to examine and to explain the techniques of a joke the joke will disappear.' Nevertheless, I believe it is useful and interesting to examine some of the characteristics of humour.

I have divided jokes and amusing remarks into different types, because you might be interested in types of humour and why we find things funny. And, of course, you can tell some of these English jokes to your friends and see whether they like them!

★ Why not learn and practise some of them and have a go!

Incongruity

What is incongruity? Here are some incongruous sights!

We laugh, or at least we smile, when we see something which is incongruous . . . usually! We don't laugh if we feel it is insulting to us or threatening to us. People often laugh if we describe an incongruous sight or incongruous behaviour. We see what is unusual and realise that it is unusual and that it is not dangerous or insulting and so we laugh with relief and with superiority.

During a carnival someone might dress in their usual clothes but wear a false nose. If the person is middle aged and wears a rather conventional and smart suit and if his face is rather serious then he might look very funny.

There was this man standing in a crowded underground train and he said to the woman standing next to him, 'Can I get you a strap to hold on to?' And she said, 'No thank you, I've got one.' And he said, 'That's my tie!'

Superiority

We are all anxious to be respected and to have importance even if it is only a little bit of importance! One way of feeling important is to feel that someone else is unimportant! So a lot of jokes are intended to make someone else seem to be foolish so that we can feel superior! In a survey in the United States more than half the things which made people laugh were jokes, put-downs, and clever remarks against other people.

Some of these types of joke are really rather cruel and undignified for the teller and the listener. Also these jokes or funny remarks often depend on stereotypes. Here is a joke based on the stereotyped idea that women talk more than men.

Two old women were heard discussing the death of one of their husbands. One woman said, 'What were his last words?' And the other replied, 'He didn't say anything. I was with him to the end.'

Here is a joke against people who want to criticise in order to feel superior.

Two men met in a park. One of them had a little dog. He boasted about his little dog saying how wonderful it was. At last the other man became impatient and said, 'Go on. Show me how clever he is.' So the man with the little dog picked up a stick and threw it into the lake which was next to them. And he told the dog to fetch it. Anyway the little dog ran along the surface of the water, picked up the stick and brought it back. 'There you are!' said the owner. 'That's nothing,' said the other. 'He can't even swim.'

Our identity in a group

If we feel superior then we feel we are important and that we have identity. We also feel that we have identity if we belong to a group – we are English, northerners, intellectuals, sporty characters, young, middle aged, or we think we are just ordinary sensible people. We often think it is funny when someone doesn't behave like other people in the group (unless we think it is insulting or dangerous). We like to be funny when we are with people we think are in our sort of group. When we make the joke and laugh we feel very much as though we are together and that we are strong.

Here are some typical jokes against people who don't belong to our group. The first joke would be for a group of men because it is against women.

American women like quiet men: they think they're listening.

This joke is for adults and against children (the child is made to seem foolish).

Mother speaking to her little boy: 'You were a good boy not to drop your sweet paper on the floor in the bus. What did you do with it?'
Little boy: 'I put it in a man's pocket.'

We smile because we belong to the group of adults and the little boy doesn't. But we think he would like to belong, so we feel OK. Many people also smile when animals are made to imitate people, for example, monkeys in clothes. We ignore their character and laugh at their failure to be really like us.

For some people the joke below is funny because it makes the porter seem stupid, and so they feel superior. However, I like the joke and feel that the porter has made a very clever remark!

A passenger in a railway station complains to a porter, 'There are two clocks in this station and they both tell different times.' And the porter replies, 'Why should we have two clocks if they tell the same time?'

In many countries there is one group of people that many people tell jokes about. In Germany people often tell jokes about the people who live in the region of East Friesland. In Sweden people often tell jokes about the people

of Norway. In each case it makes the teller and the listeners feel superior . . if they enjoy it! I don't like group identity jokes. I don't feel it is a kind or dignified way of being entertaining. But I do admit the jokes are often quite clever.

Fear

Sometimes, if we are anxious or frightened, we try to be funny and actually make people laugh because it is a relief. I believe that many of the Irish jokes which have been told in Britain in recent years are partly because people are so anxious about the unhappy situation there and because they feel so incapable of doing anything about it.

Although this may be a reason for telling jokes against the Irish I believe it can only add to the problems of the Irish and British people, so I won't give an example of an Irish joke!

Laughing at our society

Some people are critical of parts of their society. They may not like the government or the established opinions and behaviour of the majority of the people. So they tell jokes to try to make things seem to be ridiculous.

Not only is there no God, but try getting a plumber on weekends.
(Woody Allen)

(Describing a famous politician) *'How can you tell when he is lying?' 'When his lips are moving.'*

What is the difference between Capitalism and Communism? Capitalism is the exploitation of man by man; Communism is the reverse.

Laughing at ourselves

Sometimes we just want to laugh about our own behaviour when we take ourselves too seriously.

It's not that I'm afraid to die. I just don't want to be there when it happens.

I want to tell you a terrific story about oral contraception. I asked this girl to sleep with me and she said, 'No'.
(Woody Allen)

Surprise and suddenness

A lot of the jokes in this section are funny because we don't expect the ending. The ending is a surprise. Also, we like to laugh when someone in a joke is surprised, particularly if they look foolish and they aren't a very nice person!

A film starlet once went up to George Bernard Shaw, the famous playwright and author, at a party and said, 'Just imagine if we got married and our child

Barathon's propeller-driven lifebuoy (1895)

had your brains and my beauty.' And
*George Bernard Shaw replied, 'But
imagine if it had my beauty and your
brains!'*

An original idea

If an idea is very original we may smile
or laugh with admiration. And at the
same time we might laugh because we
know that it is an idea which couldn't
work. The 19th century seemed to be
full of inventors with very original
ideas . . . were they always serious?

Monsieur François Barathon of Paris
invented a machine for saving people
who have fallen into the sea. The
person sits on a rubber bag filled with
air. The rubber bag is fixed to a frame;
there is a propeller at the bottom of the
frame and at the back of the seat. The
person can turn two handles with his
feet and two with his hands and drive
the two propellers. If the wind is in the
right direction the person can also raise
a sail on the mast. And if the person
has fallen into the sea in the night he
can light a lamp which may attract the
attention of passing ships.

Some people have the ability to think
of original ideas when they are
describing things. The Irish are often
very good at creating wonderful
images. In the following case a man
wanted to describe how thin his
neighbour had become.
*She is so thin she could split hailstones
with her nose.*
Some types of joke make use of
originality as the basis of their humour.
*Question: What is a net?   Answer:
Holes tied together with string.
Question: What is an octopus?
Answer: An eight-sided cat.
Question: What is hail?   Answer:
Hard-boiled rain.*

*Question: What is it that goes 99 plonk?
Answer: A centipede with a wooden
leg.*

The illogical

If something is logical it is 'reasonable
and sensible' and in Britain an illogical
kind of humour is very common.
*Question: What would you do if you
swallowed your pen?   Answer: Use a
pencil.*

*I was travelling to London by train
when I noticed this man. Every 20
minutes he tore a sheet out of his
newspaper and rolled it into a ball.
Then he went to the window and threw
it out. Eventually I asked him what he
was doing and he said, 'If I throw balls
of newspaper out of the window every
20 minutes it keeps the elephants
away.' So I said to him, 'But there
aren't any elephants here.' And he said,
'That proves that it's a good idea.'*

*Husband: Doctor, my wife thinks she is
a chicken.
Doctor: Oh, dear. That is awful. How
long has she been like that?
Husband: Three years.
Doctor: Three years! Why didn't you
bring her to me before?
Husband: I couldn't. We needed the
eggs!*

Puns

There are many words in English
which have several different meanings.
For this reason a very common form of
English humour is based on 'punning'.
Usually people laugh with admiration
and because of their pleasure in understanding the joke and being part of it.
Puns are very difficult to understand
if English is not your first language

because you may only know one of the meanings.

Old lady: You're pretty dirty, aren't you?
Little girl: Yes, and I am even prettier clean.
('Pretty' can be used to mean 'very'. The little girl didn't understand the meaning intended by the old lady.)

Question: What is the difference between a hill and a pill? Answer: One is hard to get up and the other is hard to get down.

'Waiter, waiter! There's a hair in my soup!' 'That's all right sir, it's hare soup.'
'What do you call this?' 'That's bean soup, sir.' 'I don't care what it's been, what is it now?'

Misunderstanding

These jokes are very much like puns; they play with the different meanings in the sentences.

This joke also contains a joke against authority and a joke of improbability.
(The boss is pointing to a cigarette on the floor.) 'Is this yours Bottomley?' 'No, sir. You saw it first!'

A newspaper reporter once asked the film star, Gene Kelly, 'When did you first begin to like girls?' And Gene Kelly answered, 'As soon as I found out that they weren't boys!'

Confidence is the feeling you have when you don't know all the facts.

Middle age is when you feel as young as ever but it takes more effort.

Exaggeration

Exaggeration is sometimes funny because the idea is incongruous because it is so different.
(Describing someone who didn't want to be persuaded to do something.) 'It was like trying to drag a beetle through a barrel of glue.'

Understatement

Understatement is a traditional form of humour in Britain. The idea is to say something which is much less important than the situation. Understatements are used in some jokes but they are often used in normal conversation and not always intended to be humorous.
'I am just going outside, and may be some time.' (The last words of Lawrence Oates (1912), recorded in the diary of Robert Scott who led an expedition to the South Pole. Oates was lame with frostbite and thought he would slow down the journey of his companions, so he left the tent one night in order to die.)

The little boy's remark here is an understatement:
'Dad, what has a green and yellow striped body, six hairy legs and great big eyes on stalks?' 'I don't know. Why?' 'One's just crawled up your trouser leg!'

'Waiter, there's a dead fly in my soup.' 'Oh yes, sir. It's the hot water that kills them.'

Shaggy dog stories

There is a type of joke which is sometimes called a 'shaggy dog' story. People listen to a long joke only to find that the ending is not really very funny. *Two race horses were complaining about how tired they were. They were saying that their trainer made them work too hard. Then this dog went past and he overheard them. And he said, 'Why not pretend to be ill? I pretended to be ill and my owner gave me a holiday. And it's marvellous!' When the dog had gone one of the race horses said to the other, 'Do you think that's a good idea?' And the other one said, 'No.' And the first one said, 'Why not?' And the second one said, 'Well, who has ever heard of a dog that could talk?'*

Funny poetry

The first poem below is a limerick. Limericks are always of five lines; usually the first, second and fifth lines rhyme, and the third and the fourth.

There was a young man of Devizes,
Whose ears were different sizes.
The one that was small
Was no use at all,
But the other won several prizes.

I wish I had your picture,
It would be very nice
I'd hang it in the attic
To scare away the mice.

Money is like honey, my little sonny,
And a rich man's joke is always funny.

Clever use of the language

The future is not what it was.

We admire people who can make ideas seem very simple and who can express them very cleverly. Here is an example in which the readership of all the British newspapers is summarised in single sentences. And each sentence is a variation of each of the others. There are also other types of humour in it as well, such as 'exaggeration'.

The Times is read by the people who run the country.
The Guardian is read by the people who would like to run the country.
The Financial Times is read by the people who own the country.
The Daily Telegraph is read by the people who remember the country as it used to be.
The Daily Express is read by the people who think the country is still like that.
The Daily Mail is read by the wives of the men who run the country.
The Daily Mirror (which once tried to run the country) is read by the people who think they run the country.
The Morning Star is read by the people who would like another country to run the country.
The Sun – well, Murdoch has found a gap in the market – the oldest gap in the world.

(Quoted on the cover of F. Hirsch and D. Gordon, *Newspaper Money*, and in the *Penguin Book of Quotations*.)

27

Where would you put these jokes?

★ In which section above would you put these jokes or funny conversations? Would you need a new section? Are there different types of joke in each one?

Two people in an exhibition of modern sculpture. The sculpture is made of broken pieces of metal and broken glass. One person says to the other, 'Let's get out of here quickly. Someone will say we did it!'

Someone asked a father whether his new baby liked him. 'Oh yes, he likes me. He sleeps all day when I am not there and then he stays awake all night to play with me.'

Be unemployed, three million people can't be wrong!

This is a free country, madam. We have a right to share your privacy in a public place.

And here is the lesson I learnt in the army. If you want to do a thing badly, you have to work at it as though you want to do it well.

Talking about jokes

★ Would you divide and describe jokes like I have done in this section? Which other types of joke would you include? Do you know what makes people laugh?

Some people like to discuss questions like this, and this is why I have divided the section up according to types. If you want to be entertaining, then perhaps you could start an interesting discussion on these questions. Here are some research results you might like to use!

Laughter occurs mainly in conversations rather than as a result of jokes.
About 20% of laughter is caused by jokes.
Men tell more jokes than women (59%).
The main subjects of jokes are:
Sexual jokes (49%)
Jokes against minority groups (21%)
Jokes about unusual behaviour (19%)
Harmless jokes (11%)

Do you believe this research represents the truth for you?

AFTER LEHMA

How to tell stories

We tell people about what happened to us on the way to work; what happened to us when the boss called us in to his office; what happened to our neighbours when their daughter ran away from home.

We tell people stories at work, at home, in the café and on trains. We tell stories in noisy places; or to our children as they lie in bed.

Are stories just for children? Of course not! The radio and TV put on stories for adults every afternoon and evening.

It is important for us all to be able to describe our daily experiences or to tell stories in an interesting way.

'Whenever I try to tell anybody anything they just go to sleep! I daren't say anything.'
'If I start to tell someone a story or tell them about something that's happened, they start to look away and sometimes they even start to talk to someone else!'
'I've got a friend who seems to be able to tell people anything and make it seem interesting! I don't know how he does it!'

Aren't we all frightened of being a bore ... except bores?

What is a bore? A bore is someone who talks continually about things which don't interest you. He or she may not be boring to everyone else. It is our lack of interest which makes someone into a bore!

Why do people want to listen to other people? Why do we listen when people tell us about what has happened to them? Why do we listen to stories? Here are a few possible reasons.
★ Put them in order of importance for you.

A We like to hear about other people's problems because we realise that we are not the only ones to have problems. And we like to hear about other people's good fortune because we think it might happen to us one day.
B We like to listen to other people because it is important for us to relate to other people. It makes us feel less alone.
C We like to experience drama. And if we can experience drama without really suffering, then so much the better!
D We like to escape from our problems or our very ordinary and boring lives.

★ Would you add any other reasons why we want to listen to other people's experiences or stories?

Common interests

★ Which of these subjects might interest you if someone told you about them?
- looking after racing pigeons
- being successful at work
- trying to love a difficult person and eventually being loved by them
- making and sailing model ships

– ordinary, daily events at work
– struggling to achieve the ambition of
a lifetime
– bad luck and its effect on someone
– good luck and its effect on someone
– football training
– shopping for daily food
– being frightened by a criminal,
tricking the criminal and escaping

Pigeons and common interests

Are you interested in pigeons? If you
are then you would be interested if
someone began to speak about them.
But could someone talk about pigeons
and interest people who aren't
interested in pigeons? Surely that must
be the secret of a good storyteller? Here
is a story about pigeons!

THE PIGEON

'I've always loved pigeons. And some years
ago I managed to persuade my wife to let
me buy a few and start racing them myself.
They cost a lot of money and so it meant
that we couldn't go on holiday and that
sort of thing. It spoilt our marriage a bit,
really, but my wife never actually stopped
me so I just carried on. I learnt so much
about them I could recognise a good racer
anywhere and I bought some beauties. My
pigeons won some top races. And I even
began to make a bit of money. You see, if
people get to know that your pigeons are
winning big prizes they are prepared to pay
big prices.

Then last year I even made a profit! My
wife had been changing her attitude to the
pigeons over the last year or two anyway.
She was quite proud of all the prizes we'd
won. Then there was the travelling, she
liked that. You see someone has to take the
pigeons a long way off and release them.
Some of the trips were really nice. Last year
she went over to France. I never travelled. I
used to like to wait at home and see them

come in. I'd spend all night sometimes
waiting for them. They are so slim and
beautiful. And then they've got this
wonderful sense of direction which can
bring them back home so quickly. They'd
flown hundreds of miles sometimes
through storms or against stiff winds. And
there they'd come, tiny white birds against
those great skies. Then I'd watch them
circle round and come down onto the roof
and then onto the landing shelf. I'd look at
my watch and think, "My Goodness that's
a good time." And I'd take off the little leg
ring and push it through the machine to
record what time he'd arrived. Then my
wife would phone up and say, "Has he
arrived yet?" And we would work out if
we'd won again.

Then last year we had a disaster! One of
them got some sort of flu and died, then
they all went down. It was terrible. I had to
burn them all. We lost a fortune, of course.
And that's what my wife went on about.
But I really missed all those beautiful
creatures.

Anyway, one day I saw a pigeon for sale.
I went to see it and I knew that I was
looking at the prince of all pigeons. But the
bloke that owned him knew he was good
too. And he wanted a really high price for
him. Well, my wife and I talked about it
and decided to borrow the money. We were
sure we would get it back even on the first
big race. He just needed to grow a bit more
and get up his full strength.

So we borrowed the money and we
bought him and I was right, he was a
winner. He won several small races and
then we put him in for the big one. On this
occasion my wife didn't take him to the
start of the race, I did. She wasn't feeling
too well.

I couldn't get back home immediately so
I rang up after a few hours to see whether
he had arrived. My wife said he had arrived
and she said it was a fantastically fast time.
But she sounded strange, really odd on the
phone. And I asked her if everything was
all right. Anyway she didn't really answer
me. When I got home I found out that the

pigeon had flown the distance in a record time. But he had sat on the roof and not come down onto the shelf so my wife could take his leg ring and clock it through. Anyway she said she got so desperate because she knew he must have done a record flight that she took the air rifle and shot him down off the roof. And then she took his ring off and clocked in the time. It was a record. And we got the prize. But I've not had the heart to get any more pigeons.'

★ Which of these 'common interests' did you recognise in the story: health and survival; loving and being loved; being respected; struggling against difficulties and winning; excitement based on competition, pride, struggle, fear, beauty, bad luck, good luck, sex, sympathy, indignation, money?

You probably recognised some of these 'common interests' in the story, showing how even a story about pigeons can be interesting to people who don't particularly like pigeons. (I originally heard this story on the radio and I thought it was a true story. But I then came across a very similar story written by Carlos Martinez Moreno, *La Paloma*, referred to in *Once Upon a Time*, by John Morgan and Mario Rinvolucri.)

Looking for connections

As you talk to someone you try to connect your subject with the interests and the knowledge of your listener. If you are describing an experience or telling a story to a friend or someone you know well, you can refer to people, places and interests that your friend knows and has. You will also know if they like a more intellectual, abstract description or a more personal one.

★ Try this. Imagine you want to tell a friend or someone you know well about an experience of yours.

1 Think of a subject you know.
2 Think of someone you know who doesn't know the subject.
3 List some of the similarities and/or differences and/or connections between your subject and what the person knows, has experienced and/or cares about. List some expressions you might use.

For example, I might choose as my subject contemporary art, language teaching, unicycling, cross country running or living in Manchester. In order to explain any of these subjects I would have to look for links with what a particular person knows and cares about. Here is an example based on my experience and one of my friends:

1 Manchester and what it is like to live there.
2 My friend lives in the country. He has never lived in a city and rarely been to one.
3 In the country the day and the seasons are important. In the city they are not so important. The street lights are on all night. Many shops are lit all night.
In the city we live and work in centrally heated houses and offices in the winter. And we travel by heated cars, trains and buses. The seasons are not so important.
In the country it is often completely silent except for natural noises like the wind. In the city it is never silent; even in the middle of the night you can hear cars and trains.
In the country most people know each other. In the city most people are strangers. 'Streams of strangers pass my window!'

Here are two short descriptions of Manchester for my country friend. In each case I have chosen a country experience as a way of expressing my feelings for Manchester.

Manchester used to be one of the most prosperous industrial and commercial cities in the world. Now the 19th century buildings which dominate the centre of Manchester are like huge, deserted beehives.

The new buildings in Manchester seem to grow out of the old city like bright mushrooms on a fallen and decaying tree.

Your interests

Talk about things that you know about and, even more important, have a feeling or an opinion about. Don't worry that you may not have flown in a jet to a distant country; you may not have met any famous people and stayed with them in their country house; you may feel that your life is totally ordinary!

Everyone is different! And if you want to talk and tell stories, then concentrate on what you know and feel. Experiences which are ordinary for you can be interesting for other people if they sense that you have an opinion or a feeling about them. A dull description of the Great Wall of China is less interesting than happiness, sadness, indignation, excitement, astonishment . . . it doesn't matter how ordinary the subject is.

Character

If you care in some way about something then you will give it character when you speak about it. There are different kinds of character. For example, if you are indignant about something then your story or description will be characterised by indignation. If you feel very conscious of the importance of a person in your description, you will make him or her 'come alive'; you will describe one or two characteristics of the person. Because you know how individual they are you won't use a cliché to describe them.

Here are some clichés in English:
absent-minded professor
charming little girl
severe old teacher

Here is a one-sentence description by Woody Allen:

'Kugelmass was bald and as hairy as a bear, but he had soul.'

What a marvellous image! In one sentence we see his pathetic appearance and learn that he has 'soul', meaning character and feeling.

★ Imagine someone you know, and see if you can think of one sentence which includes a physical description and a description of their character.

Sometimes a place may be very important in your description or story, and you will feel the need to say something about it. Here is a description of a house I know well; the house is important because it is so much a part of the person who lives in it.

'The front door has green coloured glass in it. The floor is made of dark purple and brown tiles. The wallpaper is green, and wavy lines go right up to the high ceiling. The man that lives there, Jo Henshaw, rarely puts the light on and the only light comes in through the coloured glass in the front door, so it is like being at the bottom of a pond. And Jo himself looks like an eel, his bald head is so pointed and his thin body twists about so much!'

★ Can you think of a place and a person which are either very similar or strangely different?

Sometimes the actions of people tell us a lot about their character. Then it is worth describing the action in detail and you will find everybody listening to you! Here is a description of a man's action, from Roald Dahl's story *Mrs Bixby and the Colonel's Coat*.

'The husband folded his newspaper into a neat rectangle and placed it on the arm of his chair. Then he stood up and crossed over to the sideboard. His wife remained in the centre of the room pulling off her gloves, watching him carefully, wondering how long she ought to wait. He had his back to her now, bending forward to measure the gin, putting his face right up close to the measurer and peering into it as though it were a patient's mouth.'

Here is a dentist at home folding his newspaper and measuring his drink with great care. The relationship with his wife is shown because she is described as separate from her husband and watching him.

★★ You probably know many characteristic actions of your friends and neighbours. Describe a characteristic action of someone you and your friend know and see if he or she can guess who you are thinking of.

Every story must have drama

The last section was about the importance of giving character to people and places and of your feelings about them. If you can do this then you are a good and interesting 'describer' of your ideas and experiences. But what is the difference between a story and a description? I don't think it is important to look for an academic definition of each. Stories have drama and if you want to entertain someone by telling stories then you must give them drama! I will use the word 'story' to mean any description which is dramatic and interesting to the listener. You may not want to tell stories in the traditional sense, but I think you will find that the suggestions below are useful for anyone who simply wants to make his or her 'telling' interesting. And I am calling these 'tellings' *stories*.

Here are some tips for putting drama into your stories.

Contrast

If you contrast you create tension and the beginnings of drama.

Two people may have very similar aims and they may have to struggle with the same difficulties. For example, they may both want to get better jobs and they may both be poor. However, because they have different characters they will try to achieve their aims in different ways. One of them may be a likeable person and people may help him or her; the other may be lonely but hard working. So it is important in some stories to relate a person's character to what happens to them. The contrast between the way in which the two people behave provides the interest in the story.

★ Can you think of two people who have a similar aim but quite different characters?

You can also contrast a person and a place, for example: 'The delicate, gentle girl lives on the wild high moors with her father, who is a strange and silent farmer.' Can you think of such a contrast from your own experience?

Conflict

Conflict is the heart of drama.
Somebody wants something and must
struggle to get it. If you want to tell a
story make sure you:

1 Make your main person seem real
and full of character.

2 Either say what their aim is or give
your listener the impression that you
know what the aim is.

3 Describe who or what is opposing
the person and making it difficult for
them to achieve their aim. The person
might be opposed by:

– another person

– circumstance, e.g. being poor, the
climate

– bad luck, e.g. a road accident, bad
weather, a lost letter

– another part of themselves, e.g. a
person might really want to pass their
examination but might like spending
time with friends.

4 The person wins the struggle by:

– determination, bravery, etc.

– being clever

– being lucky

– help from other people

5 Keep up the excitement by
introducing new people, bad luck, etc.
for your 'hero' to struggle against. You
mustn't make it seem too easy.

The ideas above may seem rather
obvious, but if you want to be able to
tell stories and turn your experiences
into stories, you will have to practise!

★ Try this. Think of a real experience
   which has happened to you or to
   someone you know. Using the ideas
   above write down:

1 A sentence or two describing a
character.

2 A sentence describing what it is that
the person wanted.

3 A sentence or two describing who or
what made it difficult for them.

4 A sentence or two saying how they
struggled against it.

These are some of the most
important characteristics of a good
story. If you write down ten different
examples you will start to think like a
storyteller! Of course, there are more
things to a successful story than these
points, and you will find some more
ideas in the following sections.

Fact and truth

It is well known that a fisherman
always exaggerates. He says:

And people say he isn't telling the truth
because the fish wasn't as big as he
says. This is an important point for all
storytellers (and indeed for all artists)!
No description, story, painting, film,
photograph or sound recording can
represent everything. All of them must
be a selection of the information. And
the storyteller, the painter, the film-
maker all decide what they think is
important to them, and then they try to
describe that. When the fish was on the
fisherman's line he felt tremendous
excitement and he felt the powerful
pull of the fish. In his story he tries to

tell us about his excitement. He has to exaggerate the size of the fish in order to make us understand how amazed and excited he was. The truth for the fisherman was his feeling. The fact that the fish was smaller than he said is unimportant. In storytelling you must select and exaggerate in order to convey feeling and ideas.

Language

There is an English saying, 'It is not what a person says but how he says it which matters.' Your voice, your body, your gestures can remain the same or change continually and express changes of feeling and idea. Your words can be general like the word, 'nice', or more individual and specific like 'gentle'. Your expressions might be well known like, 'it was raining cats and dogs' or individual, 'the rain was pounding on the tin roof like a thousand people dancing on it with wooden legs.' You may want to create your own 'poetry' if you enjoy the sound of words.

Of course, sometimes you want to speak like everybody else and then it will seem real, but sometimes you will want to make your language rich because people enjoy it. You can use alliteration ... several words which begin with the same sound, for example, 'fat fish', 'big bus' or, more poetically, 'Western wind, when will you warm me again?' Or you can contrast sounds like, 'golden fire' and 'cool wind'. These are just a few of the characteristics of an entertaining use of language.

★ Perhaps you use language richly and poetically already. If you don't, then why not see how easily you can write down:
some original expressions
some alliterations
some words with contrasting sounds

SIMILES

You will make your language richer and you will be more entertaining if you use similes. A simile makes a comparison. For example, we might say a person is 'like a fox', meaning that he is a clever sort of person. Similes are usually introduced by words or phrases such as: *like, as if . . ., as though . . ., as . . . as, seems like . . ., than . . ,* etc. (It would be a metaphor if we said, 'He *is* a fox', meaning that the person and the fox are one and the same.) Even well-known similes add interest to a description, for example:
He works like a horse.
She sings like a bird.
She swims like a fish.
He looks like death warmed up.

An unusual simile is fresh and strong. It makes people smile as they see the connection between the experience and the idea in the simile. Here are some similes which are not very common:
angry: as angry as a corked volcano
awkward: as awkward as a cow on ice
calm: as a lake in heaven (W.S. Gilbert)
chance: as much chance as a one-armed
blind man in a dark room trying to shove a pound of melted butter into a wildcat's left ear with a red hot needle (P.G. Wodehouse)
dangerous: like playing tennis with a hand grenade (William McIlvanney)
eat: like a cement mixer (B.J. Jones)
face: like a bag of chisels

There is no reason why you shouldn't invent your own similes. It is difficult to do when you are speaking, but if you practise you will be able to do it!

★ Invent several similes for each of these words and ask your friends to choose the one they think is the best. Remember that you can either be positive or negative; in other words, you can either say that someone is 'very lonely' or that they are 'not lonely at all'.

lonely
brave
friendly
attractive
easy
happy
miserable
nervous

I have noticed that some foreigners translate common similes from their own language into English. These similes are sometimes very new to an English person. You might like to translate some well-known similes in your language into English and then try them on an English-speaking person and see what they say!

Storytelling style

In some countries the tradition of telling stories is still alive and there is a traditional style of telling stories. The storyteller's voice and the sort of language they use is traditional. But a traditional style can seem rather false in those countries where the tradition has been lost. The style you use to describe your experiences or to tell a story must be your own. Generally, in countries where there is no tradition now, the storyteller begins to tell his or her story without people realising that they are hearing one! The story arises in the conversation and seems to come out of what someone else has said. A well-known way of beginning a story is to relate it to what has just been said like this, 'That reminds me of a man I met in . . .' or 'talking of rain, that reminds me of a rainstorm in the Lake District when . . .'

If you hesitate because you can't find the right word, don't worry. Because you are searching for a particular word people will think you must be trying to say something important! Also, hesitation and making people wait can raise interest and tension!

Some people always want to interrupt your story. This is normal. It isn't because you are a bad storyteller. Usually it is better to ignore them. If other people laugh or comment, wait until they have finished, try not to look annoyed at the interruption and then continue with your story. If you aren't upset by interruptions they can help make the telling more amusing. Some people interrupt because they want to be the centre of things but, of course, other people interrupt because they are affected by your story or because they want you to explain something.

Beginnings and endings

BEGINNINGS

If you want to write a story rather than just tell it then you mustn't have a slow start. People are prepared for a story when they are reading. However, if you are telling a story during a conversation, you may have to move slowly into the story without anyone realising.

If you want to tell stories you can learn a lot from well written short stories. Here are two openings of short stories. In each case the author begins quickly, and immediately tries to capture your interest by describing a character or describing a problem or both!

In three sentences Woody Allen paints an intriguing picture of a man called Kugelmass:

Kugelmass, a professor of humanities at City College, was unhappily married for the second time. Daphne Kugelmass was an oaf. He also had two dull sons by his first wife Flo, and was up to his neck in alimony and child support.'

(*oaf:* clumsy idiot; *alimony:* money paid by a man to his former wife)

In these three sentences I can find 14 pieces of information! I have a sense of a character and a sense of his problem.

Nadine Gordimer begins her short story *You name it* with these three sentences:

'She has never questioned who her father was. Why should she? Why should I tell her?'

In these three short sentences we are introduced to three people and to a sense of a problem.

In the first few paragraphs most modern authors try to give the reader some information on:
what the story is about
who it is about
when or where it takes place

If you are telling a story and not writing one then you may not want an obvious beginning, but you should make a connection with what has gone before in the conversation. If your subject is strange or not well known to your listeners then you must help them to 'connect' with it: use similes and metaphors and comparisons which they will understand.

ENDINGS

Many short stories end with a surprise. Did you expect the ending of 'The pigeon' on page 31? Surprise endings

aren't essentia[l]
often unpleasa[nt]
listener because
However, stories,
written or just tol[d]
own experiences, sh[?]
ending of some kind.
that they have heard a[?]
experience.

If you have a clear en[ding] when you are telling a story, people will know when you have finished and will know when to laugh or look sad or to comment.

Inventing stories

I have assumed that most people just want to describe their experiences in an interesting way. However, some people might like to invent stories which aren't based on their experience. Here are a few ways in which stories can be invented:

1 Many great authors have taken existing stories and re-written them in a new way. So why shouldn't you? Why not try it? Take a short story that you know and substitute different people and places in it. You might take an old tale and set it in modern times.

2 Describe any of the features of a story, for example, a person, a setting, an aim, a problem, and then invent the other features to go with it. Here is an example: I want to write a story but I can't think of anything so I decide to describe a setting:

It was dark and it was raining steadily. It was a fine rain, almost like strands of hair wrapping wetly around the skin and hands of the people going home. It was in a city, but not in the centre where the shops are bright and full of style and show. It was in a side road of detached houses and small blocks of modern flats.

. Can you think who this
. could be about? What do they
want and what are their difficulties?
If you want to try short story writing
why not try this as a beginning?

3 Base a story on a personal advertisement in a local newspaper. Here are a
few examples from a local newspaper:

PAIR GREEN VELVET curtains, 8' drop, 112" wide, £50. 3 bar electric wall fire and surround. £45. Silvercross pram £25, kitchen table and 4 chairs, white £30, baby walker £5. ☎ 445 6373
PERSIAN RUG geometric design, blue background with gold, rust, beige, green, offers around £200. ☎ 434 2795
ELECTRIC GUITAR. Les Paul, copy and case £100. 100W custom sound, combo, amp, many features, £150 ono. Wrought iron coatstand with mirror £25. ☎ 445 0485
CRASH helmet, hockey skirt, blankets, hockey boots, suitcases, carpets, Venetian blinds, ladies shoes, skirts. 586 3280

KIND, responsible substitute mother for an eleven year old. Early mornings and evenings. Can live in during week From September for two months. 5/6 day week Archway area. Driving an advantage. 272-1193
MANDOLIN as new, with tutor books, £35 ono. ☎ 224 8017
PERSON TO PERSON introductions for friendship/ marriage, for that special someone. 01-599 8384 or PO Box 306, N19 3UP
WORKING MAN (60) would like occasional meeting with lady, must be tall. Please reply to Box No 6432, Express Office, Perrins Court, Hampstead, NW3

4 Base a story on a newspaper article.
Make the information from the article
part of a story. You must describe what
happened before and afterwards. Here
are two articles from a local newspaper:

£7.50 Start to Life Together

FIRST a little flirt in a swimming pool, then holding hands in the fishmarket, soon the first big love.

Claudia is 13 and Michael is 16 years old, they have known each other for a month and have been missing for one week with … £7.50.

Both are blonde. Claudia has beautiful, shoulder length hair. Michael has short hair. Both come from Didsbury.

'He is wonderful,' Claudia assured her mother, Mrs Ann Warbrook. 'He's 1.80 metres tall and so strong.'

Michael, the son of a painter and decorator, wants to be a seaman. 'He is humorous, self-confident and reliable,' according to his school report.

'My daughter has all the freedom she could wish for,' says Claudia's mother (42), a taxi driver. 'And I think that Michael is a really pleasant boy. Why should they want to go away without telling me?'

Claudia smashed her money box owl, took her money, and went to meet Michael for an evening out. But she hasn't returned and neither has he.

Did Michael or Claudia really run away together? Only one parent is mentioned . . . what about the husband? Perhaps he lives elsewhere and perhaps Claudia quarrelled with her mother and left to join him?

Here is another short and most innocent article. Can you imagine any drama in it?

Sydney Retires After 40 Years

POSTMAN Sydney Holt was overwhelmed by presents and gifts of money from his grateful customers when he retired last week.

Sydney, of Belfield Road, Didsbury, retired after 40 years of delivering letters in the South Manchester area.

He got a clock from his workmates, and a farewell party organised by the local Women's Institute.

His wife Jill said, 'We'd like to thank all the people who gave gifts. There were too many to mention.'

It is an innocent story! And as an innocent story it is not very interesting! But imagine if Sydney's wife had added, 'The only thing to spoil the occasion was an unexpected gift. We don't know who sent it or why and we are not prepared to say what it was. But it did spoil things a little.'

5 Base a story on magazine photographs or old family photographs or objects. You can either take one photograph of a person or a place or you can take several and try to imagine

some connection between them. Here are some examples:

6 Base your story on a sentence. You can make it the first sentence, the last sentence or a sentence in the middle of your story. Here is a sentence you could use, which I overheard on a bus: 'My husband said, "You will have to choose, you know."'

7 Just take four words and imagine a story based on them, e.g.:
car   want   weak   anxious

Be clear!

If you are telling a story, make sure the listeners understand what you are telling them. It isn't possible to give as much information when you are telling as when you are writing. The 14 bits of information in Woody Allen's description of Kugelmass would be lost if they were given in three spoken sentences.

People who tell stories often repeat the main ideas in different ways. Once the listeners have got an idea of the main characters, their aims and problems, and what the story is about, the storyteller can go faster. And the good teller watches the listeners to see if they look confused and then adapts the story to the listeners.

Learning stories to tell

In spite of television, radio, books and magazines, people still like to be told stories! If you don't want to invent stories to tell why not learn some?

Look for stories in which the characterisation of people, their aims, their problems and what happens are clear. Don't take a story in which the language is subtle and the relationship between the people is more important than the actions.

But how can you remember the story? One technique is to summarise the story and to write the summary down. John Morgan and Mario Rinvolucri call these 'story skeletons' (in their book *Once Upon A Time*). Roald Dahl's short stories are wonderful ones to re-tell because there are usually very few people in the stories, their characters, aims, difficulties and conflicts are always clear and often amusing. (There are several writers whose short stories are fairly easy to learn and to tell, for example, Edgar Allan Poe (1809–1849); Guy de Maupassant (1850–1893); O. Henry (1867–1910); Ian McEwan (born 1948).)

Here is a story skeleton of *Mrs Bixby and the Colonel's Coat* by Roald Dahl, which I have used to help me remember the story.

– Mr Bixby is a dentist and cares more about his work than his wife.

– Every month Mrs Bixby tells her husband that she is going to see her old aunt, but she really goes to see her lover . . . a rich old colonel.

– Then after one visit, the colonel gives

her a beautiful black mink coat which is worth a lot of money. He also gives her a note which says that he can't see her again.

– She realises that she can't take the coat home so she puts it into a pawn shop and takes the ticket home.

– When she gets home she tells her husband that she found the pawn ticket in the taxi.

– Her husband says he will take the ticket to the pawn shop and they can find out what the object is.

– She is very excited. He phones her from his office and tells her to come immediately. He tells her to close her eyes and he will give her a surprise. She assumes it will be the coat. But it isn't, it is a horrid old fur scarf. Of course she can't say anything!

– Outside the office, in the corridor, she passes her husband's secretary who is wearing the magnificent fur coat!

★ Practise making story skeletons from short stories, films and television programmes.

Amazing stories

There is a type of story which is easy to learn, easy to tell and is always entertaining; this type of story is sometimes called a modern legend. A legend is: 'a popular story handed down from earlier times whose truth has not been proved'.

Ten years ago I was told the story below. Since that time I have heard the same story told in Canada and in Germany. I once asked a group of 60 people from 30 countries how many had heard the story and 20 of them had! Some of the 20 people were convinced that it was a true story. In the following version, which I was told, the people are Danish and the country is Italy. When I heard the story in Canada, the people were American and the country was Mexico. Perhaps you know another version of this story?

GRANDMA IN THE TENT

A Danish family were on a camping holiday in the South of Italy. There were the two parents, their two children and the rather elderly Grandmother. Tragically, the Grandmother became ill and died, very quickly.

They didn't know what to do. They couldn't speak Italian and they didn't have much money. Their holiday was nearly finished, so they decided they wouldn't tell the police.

They decided, instead, to wrap the Grandmother in the tent, to tie her on the roof of their car and to drive home to Denmark. They drove day and night until they reached the North of Italy. They felt very tired and decided to stay the night in a hotel in a small town. They left the tent and the Grandmother on the top of the car. Next morning when they left the hotel, they found that the car had been stolen!

★ Have you ever heard this story?
Have any of your friends heard it? You can tell this kind of story to one friend or to a group of friends and they will always be interested. After telling it you can say that you don't know if it is really true, and then start a discussion about 'modern legends'. You can say there are many more. And here are some examples!

THE NUDE BIRTHDAY PARTY

Modern legends are always told as though they have happened recently and to a friend of a friend. In fact, many of them have been told for years; the story below has certainly been told for at least 60 years. It is interesting to collect and to exchange these different versions and to compare with other people when and where they heard their version.

It was this businessman's birthday. He wasn't feeling too good about it anyway and then neither his wife nor his children even said, 'Happy Birthday.' It was as if they had forgotten it altogether. But when he got to work his secretary wished him 'Happy Birthday' and suggested they should have a birthday lunch together. He had always wanted to get on friendlier terms with his secretary so he was very pleased. They had lunch in a rather smart restaurant and then his secretary said, how about going back to her place for a coffee. This made him pretty excited . . . she had been very friendly during their lunch and he couldn't believe his good fortune. They drove back to her house; she took him into the sitting room and poured him a whisky. She said she wanted to go into her bedroom to put on some nicer clothes. He thought, this is it! As soon as she had gone out he took all his own clothes off and finished off his whisky. Then she called out from the next room, 'OK, you can come in now!' He flung the door open, ran in and found the room full of his colleagues and his family singing 'Happy Birthday to You.'

NUDE IN THE BASEMENT

This woman was down in her basement putting her washing into the washing machine. She noticed that the dress that she was wearing was rather dirty so she decided to wash that as well and took it off. It was a really hot day and she was wearing nothing underneath. Then she noticed that the pipes under the ceiling were dripping condensation water on her. She had just washed her hair so she put on her son's baseball helmet to keep the water off. A few minutes later she heard a cough behind her! She turned round and there was this gas meter man. He looked a bit nervous and said, 'I hope your team wins, lady.'

THE GHOSTLY HITCHHIKER

I met this guy who told me an amazing story. He was touring Scotland on a motorbike by himself. One late afternoon he was on the road between Aberdeen and Elgin. He was travelling along, miles from any village, when he saw a really attractive girl standing by the road, hitchhiking. Anyway, he stopped and said he would give her a lift to Elgin. She got on and he drove off. He said he liked having her on the back, it was nice company. But after a time he forgot that she was there. Suddenly he remembered her, but he realised that he couldn't feel her knees pressing against him! He felt behind him but . . . she wasn't there.

He said he felt frightened out of his life! He felt cold all over. He thought she must have fallen off the back. So he turned round and raced back along the road. He didn't find her. He went to see if she had crawled into a field or something. But he didn't find her. So he began to think that she might have been picked up by someone else. He said he felt terrible. And he felt frightened.

Anyway, he drove on towards Elgin and didn't see anyone until he came to a pub. He decided to stop so that he could talk to someone and he thought he ought to tell the police. He went into a pub and talked to the barman. He told the barman what had happened. He said the barman didn't seem to be at all surprised. He just carried on drying the glasses.

Then the barman said, 'You're not the first person to come in here and tell the same story. That girl you think you picked up died seven years ago . . . in a motorbike accident.'

THE VOLKSWAGEN

There was this man driving home late one night in Wakefield. He stopped at some traffic lights, right in the middle of the town. Suddenly, some drunken young men came along. They surrounded the car and then they began to push it from side to side.

Then one of them got hold of the back and began to lift the car and to bounce it. Anyway, he got a bit frightened and he decided he would drive off. So he accelerated and drove off at high speed.

He got home safely and didn't think any more about the experience. The next day he took the car to his garage and asked them to give it a general service. He then went to his office on foot. Later that morning he received a telephone call: the call was from the garage. The garage man said, 'Can you come down immediately, it is rather important?' He said, 'Why? I'll come down at lunchtime.' Anyway, the garage man seemed to be very anxious and he said he couldn't discuss the problem on the phone and he said he wanted to talk to him before he talked to the police!

So the man went to the garage. He was asked to go into the office. Then the manager opened up a rough ball of old newspaper. Inside was a finger. The manager said they had found the finger inside the engine grill, stuck there! He said they had wanted to show it to him before telling the police.

The finger probably belonged to one of the young men who had shaken the car in Wakefield the night before.

THE SECOND HAND CAR

There was a young couple who wanted to buy a second hand car. One day they saw a second hand car for sale in a garage. It was very cheap. They thought there must be something wrong with it. But the salesman said the engine was in excellent condition.

Anyway, they bought the car and drove it home and they were very pleased with it. There seemed to be nothing wrong with it at all. After several weeks they noticed a stain on the driver's seat. It was only a little stain but they didn't like it. After a day or two they noticed that the stain had grown bigger. They tried to clean it off and they managed to get rid of most of it. But in a few days it had come back again. They cleaned it off but, once more, the stain

came back . . . and this time it covered the whole of the seat . . . it was a colour like pale rust.

They became so upset about the stain that they put a new cover on the seat. But this didn't make any difference. The stain came through.

At last they took the car back to the garage. The salesman saw them coming and said, 'You want to sell it back, don't you?' They were astonished. 'It's the seat isn't it? There's nothing wrong with the car but someone had an accident in that car and the stain where they died always comes back.'

★ Tell these stories and I am sure you will hear many more!

Final tips

If you aren't used to talking about your experiences and your feelings you may feel that no one wants to listen. Not everyone will want to listen. That is normal. Do your best to choose the right story for the right person and tell it at the right time!

Don't get irritated or depressed if people don't listen or interrupt you. This happens to every teller. If you try to continue with your story you must continue with the same feeling as before and not sound irritated or depressed! Watch the listener, and if he or she speaks, listen carefully. Then you will know if they are interested, getting confused, or getting bored!

Develop your confidence by telling stories in an easy situation. For example, when you are on a train with a friend or when you have a coffee break at work. Don't choose a time when there are a lot of people around and a lot of distractions.

How to get people talking

Interpreting dreams

It is very boring to listen to stories about other people's dreams, but it is enjoyable to tell them. If you want to be entertaining, don't describe your dream but listen to other people's dreams and then amaze them by your knowledge of what they mean and what the latest theories are. If you want to master this subject and get yourself top prize, then remember a few famous dreams or even a few quotations.

Dream research

It is always impressive if someone can describe recent research into a subject. And it is interesting as well! *The Sunday Times* did some research into dreams. Twenty five thousand people answered the questions! Here are some of their main findings.

★★ Ask your friends the same questions, see what they reply, and then tell them the results of the research.

1 *How often do you dream?*
Some people thought that they never dreamed or hardly ever dreamed. Only a third of the men and nearly half of

the women thought that they dreamed several times a night. (In fact, research shows that everyone dreams quite frequently every night.)

2 *Do you enjoy your dreams?*
Most people replied that they did. More women said they had nightmares than men.

3 *Have you ever had 'déjà vu'?*
(The French expression 'déjà vu' is used in English to refer to an experience that we think we have had before in exactly the same form.) About 80% of the people had experienced déjà vu.

4 *Do you have anxiety dreams?*
78% of the women and 66% of the men had anxiety dreams.

5 *Do you dream in colour?*
Over half the men and women said they dreamed in colour.

6 *Do you ever have sexual dreams?*
85% of the men and 72% of the women said they had sexual dreams.

7 *Do you ever dream about the future?*
31% of the women and 26% of the men.

8 *Do you ever read in your dreams?*
13% of the women and 10% of the men.

9 *Do you ever find money in your dreams?*
24% of the men and 17% of the women.

10 *Do you ever have violent dreams?*
49% of the men and 44% of the women.

11 *Do you ever fall in your dreams?*
About 75% of men and women said they sometimes dream of falling.

12 *Are you ever chased in your dreams?*
69% of the men and 76% of the women said they were sometimes chased in their dreams.

Modern theories about dreams

As you can see from the *Sunday Times* research there are a lot of misunderstandings about dreams. So here are a few discoveries made by scientists in recent years. This kind of information always makes a conversation tick along nicely. You can put the ideas as questions if you like.

HOW OFTEN DO WE DREAM?

We all dream many times every night but we don't usually remember our dreams. If we do remember our dreams, they are usually the last ones that we had before waking up.

OUR MOVING EYELIDS

Other people know when we are dreaming because they can see our eyelids moving. If they wake us up at that moment we will remember our dream. Research by Dr Keitman at the University of Chicago has shown this. He has also tried waking people up when their eyelids aren't moving, and they have told him that they weren't dreaming!

However, blind people don't move their eyelids when they dream. This is because they can't see anything in their dreams.

HOW LONG DO DREAMS LAST?

Ten minutes to half an hour. They are not over in a moment as many people believe.

DO WE NEED TO DREAM?

Yes. If a person is prevented from dreaming but allowed to sleep he or she becomes very upset. (The person can be woken up every time their eyelids begin to move.)

Why do we dream?

There are several theories. One theory is that we need continuous experience or we will become insane. Research has shown that we become very upset if we are left in a room unable to touch, see or hear. When people try to do this their minds begin to hallucinate or wander. Possibly, then, we can't sleep without dreaming part of the time.

Another theory: we spend most of our day thinking about practical matters, shopping, getting to work, seeing our friends, etc. We spend very little of our time thinking about our deep anxieties, fears, and hopes, although these are very important. When the mind doesn't have to think about everyday matters it is free to think about these deeper concerns, and it doesn't have to be logical and 'sensible' because it doesn't have to communicate to other people. For example, time is unimportant in dreams. If something happened to you ten years ago and something else yesterday then it doesn't matter if they are combined. Also, if you haven't experienced something but would like to, then it can be real in your dream. Very often your deeper minds don't seem to have words in them and we have to represent our anxieties, fears and hopes through pictures.

Freud, Adler and Jung

Someone is certain to refer to Freud, Adler and Jung in the conversation and it would be a good idea if you knew what each of these psychologists believed and said. Bits of information of this kind are always interesting and make other people talk; they often want to agree or disagree.

FREUD

Freud (1856–1939) believed that the deep, unconscious mind has a powerful influence over the conscious mind. He believed that the conscious mind tries to control and cover up the enormous feelings which have such power, and he thought that the unconscious feelings which we struggle to cover up are largely sexual.

Today we may feel that it is a bit of a joke to think that everything we do has a sexual explanation! However, as the *Sunday Times* research showed, most people said they had sexual dreams sometimes.

Freud believed that the conscious mind would not allow the unconscious mind to express its wishes in a clear kind of way, so the unconscious mind had to symbolise its feelings. He thought that all long pointed objects represent the male: sticks, umbrellas, trees, knives, etc., and that all hollow objects represent the female: boxes, cupboards, ovens, ships, rooms, etc.

ADLER

Adler (1870–1937) worked with Freud for nine years, but then he left Freud because he felt that people were not motivated only by sex. He thought that we want to find our own personal strength and nature, and that we want to dominate and control other people. He believed that our problems are caused by having to learn to live with other people. The idea of an 'inferiority complex' and a 'superiority complex' is associated with Adler.

JUNG

Jung (1875–1961) was also a friend of Freud and worked with him. However, he too developed his own ideas about people. Jung was interested in world religions and in mystical and spiritual ideas. He believed that our personalities are divided into three parts: the conscious, the unconscious and the 'collective unconscious'. He thought that we all share the same 'collective unconscious' and he studied religions and beliefs all over the world to prove it. He found that there are heroes and magicians and fairies and dragons in stories everywhere, and he believed that these heroes, etc. represent our wish to be brave and good, our need for help against difficult problems and our fear of the unknown and the frightening within ourselves. He called these general ideas 'archetypes'.

He had another theory which is useful when you want to interpret a dream. He believed that every man has within him the characteristics of a woman: imagination, poetry, gentleness. He called this other, inside person the 'anima' of a man. And he said that in every woman there is an 'animus' which is aggressive, forceful and decisive. If a woman dreamed of a man Freud would say that she was wishing for a lover, but Jung might say that she was dreaming of the animus part of herself, or she was dreaming of an archetype of a hero or evil person, etc.

The language of dreams

If you can understand the language of dreams you will be very popular . . . unless you give someone bad news! In fact it is very difficult to find a clear meaning behind a dream, and usually the only person who can really find the meaning is the person who had the dream. It is true that we all share many of the same anxieties, fears and hopes and it is also true that we use some of the same symbols for expressing these feelings. Some of these feelings and the common symbols which represent them are described on page 48. But the particular balance of feelings is individual to us, and we also use symbols for these feelings which are only meaningful to us. These personal symbols obviously can't be looked up in a book!

If you want to help someone to understand their dream, explain that they are the only person who can really do it. However, it is important to listen and ask questions. Help the person to find connections. Writing down dreams is often helpful.

★ Try it yourself! Tonight when you go to bed make sure you have a pen and paper near you. When you wake up in the morning, write down your dream, including every detail and how you felt about it. Even as you describe your dream you may get a feeling about the meaning of it.

Your personal symbols

What do you connect the object with in your past experience? In your dream you may see a chair. What sort of chair is it? Do you recognise the chair? Perhaps it is the chair that your father uses a lot. The chair might represent or symbolise your father in this dream.

Perhaps you connect holidays with going to France. If so, you may represent your feeling of freedom with a French building or a French person. This is an example of your private symbolism which only you can interpret.

METAPHORIC SYMBOLS

Abstract ideas like love or fear can't be seen; they have to be represented. They can be represented by objects or symbols, for example, a ring or a heart. We do this in language too, for example, in similes, 'He is as strong as a lion,' and metaphors, 'He is a lion.' So if you dream of a lion, perhaps it symbolises someone in your life.

VISUAL SIMILARITY

You may see a golden light in your dream. Perhaps that golden light is like the golden light which shines around the golden hair of someone you know? You may not want to dream directly and openly about someone so you choose one of their characteristics and then join it to someone else. This person might seem to be a total stranger and this may be why we sometimes dream about people whom we think are not important to us.

You may dream about something which represents something bigger. For example, in real life, a picture of a bicycle on a road sign represents all bicycles. Correspondingly, a small problem in a dream might represent your worry about endless difficulties.

Symbols we share with others

In this section some of the main symbols that many of us share are

47

described. However, this doesn't mean that these images definitely mean the same for everyone all the time.

For each image there may be several different meanings, in the same way as many words have several meanings. The person you are talking to will probably know which explanation applies to them, although they may not want to tell you!

★★ Try the ideas on someone you know. Ask if they ever dream of these things.

FLYING

Perhaps you have an inferiority complex, which means that you feel inferior to other people. For example, 'I often fly in my dreams. And people are down below and look up at me. And they are amazed. It is very nice actually.'

Perhaps another explanation for flying is that we are trying to escape from our problems! For example, 'I have these dreams when I fly incredibly high. I can't even see the earth and certainly no people. And I seem to soar higher and higher but I'm not frightened of falling at all! I don't have these flying dreams when I don't have a lot of work to do.'

FALLING

Falling means failing or, at least, lowering oneself, so most falling in dreams probably represents fear of failure.

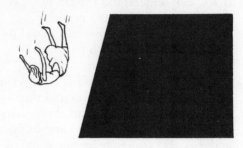

CLIMBING

You are desperately or, at least, determinedly trying to achieve success. Are your feet slipping? Perhaps you feel it is very difficult. Perhaps you fear failure?

BEING CHASED

Perhaps there is something you want to avoid? Is something haunting you? Perhaps you think you have done something wrong? Is a person following you? They may represent the ideas that you wish to escape from. Are you being chased by wild animals? Perhaps they represent aggressive characteristics in yourself which you want to escape from?

MISSING A TRAIN/BUS/BOAT/PLANE

The expression 'Don't miss the boat' means don't miss an opportunity for success. Perhaps missing the boat is your fear of failure and getting behind everyone else.

NOT BEING ABLE TO GET OFF THE TRAIN

Perhaps you are frightened of getting to your destination. Perhaps you have started something which you can't stop, and feel out of control.

LOOKING FOR A ROOM OR A HOUSE

You might be looking for a home, somewhere to be comfortable and loved. Perhaps you want to find yourself and be less confused about life. It might be that you want to get married. The house may represent you. Different things which happen in the house may represent different areas of your interests. If you don't know where to go in the house perhaps you don't know what you should do with your life. Work to be done on the house may represent your need to 'repair yourself' or to 'repair your family'.

FIRE

Fire may represent the warmth of your emotions, but it may also represent your hopes being destroyed. A fire out of control could be your fear of being out of control.

A POLICEMAN

The policeman might be the representation of your conscience.

A TRAMP

This may represent a part of you which you are ashamed of.

A BABY

You may want to have a baby! However, it may represent your wish to make something new and perfect.

A CAR

If you are driving you want to be in control of your life. If you are being driven you want someone else to look after you.

A CAT

A cat may represent, for you, mysterious feminine qualities of imagination and intuition. By the way, in Britain, black cats are lucky.

Some traditional beliefs

All the interpretations given above are reasonable, although they don't apply to every person. However, you will find that some people will say the most extraordinary things! Here are some examples of traditional beliefs which we might not find so reasonable today.

Animals   If they are calm then you will be successful in business. If they are hostile you will do badly in business!

Bath   If the bath is empty you must keep calm. If you are taking a bath then you will be unhappy!

Carpet   You will have good luck!

Cat   You will be deceived!

Dog   This will bring you good luck if it is friendly, particularly if it is a large one!

This is a totally different approach to the interpretation of dreams. Do you think these traditional interpretations are helpful? They certainly might lead to a lively argument.

Can dreams predict the future?

Some people believe that dreams can predict the future, and they will produce evidence for their belief. Jung claimed that he had dreams which predicted the future:

'I dreamed about a death in my wife's family. I dreamed that my wife's bed was a deep hole in the ground with stone walls. It was a grave. Then I heard a deep sigh, as if someone were giving up the ghost. Someone who looked like my wife sat up in the hole and floated upwards. The person wore a white gown covered in curious black symbols. I woke up and then woke my wife. We looked at the time. It was three o'clock in the morning. The dream was so curious that I thought it must symbolise a death. At seven o'clock we received the news: my wife's cousin had died at three o'clock in the morning.'

Jung also dreamed of his mother's death and received the news the next morning.

Abraham Lincoln dreamed of his own death. One evening he was rather quiet; rather sad and downcast. His wife kept asking him what was wrong, and at last he told her. He talked about dreams for a while and then he told her that a recent dream had upset him, which he described to her.

In the dream everything seemed to be very still around him, and it was like death. He could hear people crying and he was determined to find out what was happening. He went from room to room in the White House until he reached the East Room, where he saw a dead body lying wrapped in funeral sheets. He asked, 'Who is dead?' And the people replied, 'The President. He was killed by an assassin!' Then the people started crying again very loudly and Lincoln woke up.

A few days later Lincoln was shot and killed by John Wilkes Booth while he was at the theatre.

Adolf Hitler was a soldier in the German army during World War 1. He said that one night he was sleeping in a trench for protection when he dreamed he heard a voice. The voice told him to leave the trench immediately. He did so, even though his comrades told him to stay. A moment later a bomb fell on the trench and all his comrades were killed.

Many less famous people than Jung and Abraham Lincoln have had dreams predicting the future. Many people say they have learned which horse is going to win a big race, for example. One woman dreamed that she was looking for her little child and calling, 'Come here my love!' The next day My Love won the famous Derby race. According to the newspapers she predicted many winners during a period of about four years.

This is a topic of conversation which is guaranteed to be interesting. Some people will be interested because they will enjoy describing their own experiences or those of other people. Some people will enjoy making fun of the idea!

★★ When you and your friends discuss whether dreams can predict the future you might like to use these questions:
− How many people dream of things which don't come true?

− If dreams can predict the future, does that mean that everything we do is determined?
And this could lead to another good conversation!

Practise interpreting

MRS X'S DREAM

Mrs X bought her own business. Although it was only a small business it worried her a lot. She never seemed to have enough money and she felt very lonely: she had no one to talk to about it. During that time and, in fact, until she sold the business she used to have a dream regularly.

'I used to dream that I was running away and that someone was chasing me. I thought it was only one person but I could never be sure, it might have been more . . . I think it was a man but I never really knew. And then I often saw an older woman than myself and she used to stand there with her arms folded and she always looked rather angry or disapproving. And then, just when I was really frightened I would suddenly find I could fly and I used to fly right up into the air. It was marvellous really. I could see the woman down below but it didn't matter any more that she might be angry. And, although I couldn't see anyone else below I felt really pleased with myself and was sure that everyone was rather envious!'

★ Which of the ideas in this section would you use to interpret this dream?

I have written three interpretations below. Each interpretation is based on the ideas of Jung, Adler or Freud.
★ Which is which do you think? (Answers on page 64.)
1 Quite clearly Mrs X was very worried about her business. She felt

that she was being chased by her problems. She thought these might be men because so many of her business associates were men. She ran desperately away and felt that her mother would be angry with her if she got into some sort of trouble. Then she flew away and managed to get on top of her problems and even felt rather superior.

2 Mrs X was certainly concerned about her business. However, the business worries only made her real worries more severe. Her real worry was that she didn't know what to do in life. She was trying to be a businesswoman but she didn't think this was what she wanted to do. She ran away, chased by all the different choices of what she might do in life. But she always saw the other part of herself: this was an older sensible person who really did know what should be done. Unfortunately Mrs X could not find out what this should be so she entered into the heaven of infinity.

3 Mrs X had never married. She bought a business in order to have the power of a man. At the same time she knew that she was really running away from making a relationship with a man. The older woman with folded arms represented herself as she would become; old, lonely and unloved. She imagined she was with a man, at last, by flying up into the air to carefree happiness.

Ideas from famous people

If you choose the right moment a quotation about dreams might amuse your friends!

'We show life neither as it is nor as it ought to be, but as we see it in our dreams.'
(Anton Chekhov)

'So if I dream I have you, I have you. For, all our joys are but fantastical.'
(John Donne)

'No, there is nothing half so sweet in life
As love's young dream.'
(Thomas Moore)

'He is a dreamer; let us leave him: pass.'
(William Shakespeare, *Julius Caesar*)

'In dreaming, the clouds methought would open and show riches ready to drop upon me; that, when I waked I cried to dream again.'
(William Shakespeare, *The Tempest*)

'I dreamed in a dream I saw a city invincible to the
attacks of the whole of the rest of the earth.
I dreamed that was the new city of Friends.'
(Walt Whitman)

'All right, my lord creator, Don Miguel, you too will die and return to the nothing whence you came. God will cease to dream you!'
(Miguel de Unamuno)

Telling fortunes

Imagine that you have met someone you like, and you want to have some fun. You don't want to be too serious. You can talk about their stars or hands or their dreams, and they will love it! They may not believe anything you say but you will both have a good time, and you will get to know each other better. Some people really believe that

the stars do predict their future, so you must be careful not to upset them! All you need is a bit of information and a bit of imagination.

The stars

A little knowledge will take you a long way! Astrologers, the experts who can read the stars, must know exactly when you were born. They want to know the year, the month, the day and the hour when you arrived. They look at their books and they find out where the sun and the stars were at that precise moment. They can then tell you all about your character and they can tell you about your future. In some parts of the world politicians and business people will not make a major decision until they have been to an astrologer.

You can't compete with an astrologer! But you can learn a little about the character of each of the star signs. Look at your friend's face when you describe their character. They may look serious or they may smile but they will listen!

KNOW THE STAR SIGNS AND SURPRISE YOUR FRIENDS

★ You can test these descriptions. Think of someone you know and look up their star sign. Is it true? Another way of testing the descriptions would be to think of someone you know but whose birthday you don't know. Read all the star sign descriptions and decide which one seems the best. Then ask the person the date of his or her birthday and see whether you have chosen their correct star sign!

gemini
The Twins
May 20 to June 21
You have a lot of interests and you do many things. You are intelligent but you find it difficult to make decisions. You are a good talker but sometimes you bore people to death! You have opinions on everything and anything. You think rather superficially and never enjoy studying in depth. You are attractive to a lot of people of the opposite sex. You like to have a lot of friendships and enjoy making new friends.

cancer
The Crab
June 21 to July 22
You are like the crab, you have a hard outside and a soft inside. You have too much emotion and you go inside your shell if your feelings are hurt. You are like Taurus because you can work so hard and with such determination. You are very generous, perhaps too generous. You know how to advise other people but you aren't very good at advising yourself!

leo
The Lion
July 22 to August 22
Many great leaders are Leos! You are confident, and you expect to lead. You are an excellent organiser. You expect to be the centre of attention, you expect praise and you always expect the largest and the best of everything. You like people to envy you and you expect gratitude from friends and from people you help. You must remember to be a kindly king or queen! Be careful of people who say nice things to you. They are flattering you.

virgo
The Virgin
August 2 to September 23
You are ambitious and patient. You study hard and you like to gain a lot of knowledge. You are careful with your money, some people think you are mean. People like you. However, you do get upset about little matters and lose some friends because of that. You like detail. And you like clear and careful thinking. Many bachelors and spinsters are Virgos.

libra
The Scales
September 23 to October 23
You like to think clearly. And you are happiest when you are surrounded by similar kinds of people. You are creative . . . perhaps you act in the theatre, or paint, dance, sing or write poetry. You don't like doing boring work. Your emotions change a lot: sometimes you are happy and the next moment you feel sad. You work hard when you want to understand something but then, when you do understand it you lose all interest. You are friendly and people like being with you.

scorpio
The Scorpion
October 23 to November 22
You have a strong mind and a strong body. You can

make decisions and you like working by yourself. You like to be the boss. You like to lead even if you aren't qualified to be the leader. You are a perfectionist . . . you like everything you do to be perfect. And you expect everybody else to be perfect as well!

sagittarius

The Archer
November 22 to
December 21
You are extremely generous. You are open to other people even if they have very different ideas. You like a comfortable home but you also enjoy travelling and you want the freedom to go wherever you want and to do whatever you wish. You want freedom of expression and of love and you are willing to give the same freedom to your friends. You like working hard and you are always anxious to finish what you have begun. You enjoy laughing and telling jokes.

capricorn

The Sea Goat
December 21 to January 20
You are a serious person. You should try to be a little less serious and then you would be happier. You can work very hard and you can be very sensible. For these reasons you should do well in business. You must learn not to worry about little things. You won't marry when you are young because you will be frightened of marrying the wrong person. But when you do marry you will be happy.

aquarius

The Water Bearer
January 20 to February 19
You have wonderful ideas. You don't like imitations of things; you are often interestingly dressed and well ahead of fashion. You are a good clear thinker, perhaps even a philosopher.

You are more interested in people generally than in individuals, which can create problems; however, people can depend on you. But you are very unhappy when you can't depend on a friend! You should show your feelings more. If you like someone then you must learn to show it.

pisces

The Fishes
February 19 to March 21
You are kind and generous and you like people. Although you like people you don't trust them. You, yourself are not always to be trusted. You are like the fish of your sign . . . you are slippery and sly. You feel misunderstood and badly treated. You are an escapist. You see the world as you would like it to be and not as it is. You must learn to concentrate.

aries

The Ram
March 21 to April 19
You are very independent. You don't like working for other people. You have a lot of energy. And you like doing a lot of new things. You are courageous and fearless and you expect to do well. In fact you expect to come first in everything you try to achieve. You have a lot of enthusiasm but you must learn to look before you leap! Don't jump into marriage and then spend your life regretting it!

taurus

The Bull
April 19 to May 20
You work hard, you are practical, dependable and you achieve a lot. Nothing can stop you when you want to achieve something. So people like you to help them. You could build a big and happy family or a good business. You don't like new ideas. You are rather conventional. You need safety and security, without them you are anxious, tense and frightened. You should learn to consider all the information first.

The numbers know

Numerology will give you an entertaining 20 minutes!

You: Did you know that your name is you?

Your friend (puzzled): Sorry, I didn't hear you correctly. I thought you said, your name is you.

You: I did and it is!

Your friend: What do you mean?

You (with a mysterious smile): Your name controls the number which is so important in your life. Look, I'll show you . . .

Now write out the numbers 1 to 9. Then write the letters A to I beneath the numbers, then the letters J to R beneath them, then the letters S to Z. Then write out your friend's name and the matching number for each letter.

Add the numbers together. Then add the digits of each number together. Then add the new numbers together for both names if you have used two names. And finally add the digits together of the final number . . . and that is your number.

THE NUMBER TWO IS IMPORTANT IN YOUR LIFE!

This is what the numbers mean:

1 You want to be the boss. You are a strong and a creative person. You want to organise everything and everybody and you don't want to recognise difficulties.

2 You are romantic, kind and helpful. You would be a good teacher or a nurse. You are diplomatic. Your heart rules your head.

3 You like business rather than a social life. Perhaps you think about things too much. You are a bit shy and you should work hard to develop friendships.

4 You are a practical person and you are often rebellious and unconventional. You are not very interested in material possessions, and you sometimes feel isolated from your friends.

5 You are nervous and anxious. Sometimes you feel a bit hopeless and sometimes you feel very hopeful. You must try to be more determined to finish things once you have started them.

6 You are peaceful and you are kind to others. You would be an excellent father or mother. You are strong when

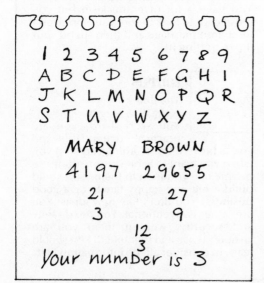

```
1 2 3 4 5 6 7 8 9
A B C D E F G H I
J K L M N O P Q R
S T U V W X Y Z

MARY      BROWN
4197      29655
  21        27
   3         9
        12
         3
Your number is 3
```

you have the right companion but you are weak when you are by yourself.

7 You like being alone. You are a very serious person; you like to think and to look after yourself. Sometimes people don't understand you. You should work hard to make your friendships grow.

8 You like business success, and you like to have expensive objects like cars, video recorders, etc. You are probably not an artist.

9 You are very emotional. You want to trust people. You listen carefully to other people and you try to understand their ideas. Because you have the highest number you have all the good characteristics of the other numbers!

HE'S HAVING ONE OF HIS UP DAYS!

Your difficult days

We sometimes use the expression 'ups and downs'. For example, we might say, 'Oh, he's all right but he does have his ups and downs!' We mean that the person is sometimes happy and sometimes unhappy, sometimes confident and sometimes rather unsure of things, and there may be no obvious reasons.

★ Do you have 'ups and downs'?

How often do you have them? Recent research shows that perhaps there are reasons that we should know about.

Swissair is one of the safest airlines in the world. Swissair don't allow a pilot and co-pilot who have the same 'critical days' to fly together. In Zurich, Switzerland, bus drivers don't drive on their 'critical days', and accidents have been cut by 50%.

In Kyoto and Osaka, Japan, during a five year period, 59% of accidents by bus and taxi drivers occurred on their 'critical days'. When the Ohmi Company explained the idea of critical days to the drivers accidents fell by 50% the next year. In one year the Ohmi bus drivers travelled four million kilometres and didn't have a single accident.

CRITICAL DAYS

Swissair, the Zurich City Corporation and the Ohmi Company in Japan believe that people's ups and downs occur regularly, and they can establish when their pilots and drivers will feel 'down'. 'Down' days can be dangerous! If you are driving you may misjudge distances and speeds and not concentrate, and if you are making important decisions about your life you may also make a serious mistake.

If the theory – called the Biorhythm theory – is true it is obviously very important indeed, but not everyone is convinced. Some people say that it isn't helpful if you are told that a certain day is going to be a bad day. They say that the knowledge will make it into a bad day for you!

★ But you should decide whether the idea is useful or not. Why not work out when your critical days are and then see how you feel?

★★ If you work out the critical days for yourself and for someone else you can then compare your experiences and decide together whether the system is useful.

When are my critical days?

Here is the theory:
You have 'ups and downs' physically, intellectually and emotionally. These 'ups and downs' follow three different rhythms, which begin when you are born.
The physical rhythm lasts 23 days.
The intellectual rhythm lasts 33 days.

The emotional rhythm lasts 28 days. When two or three rhythms cross on their average line you have a critical day. (Even one rhythm crossing the average line might give you a critical day.)

Judy Garland killed herself on June 21. On that day her emotional rhythm crossed the average line; her intellectual rhythm crossed the average line the day before and her physical rhythm was 'down', it was below the average line.

Find your critical days

Here is the technique. I have included an example . . . myself! I have worked out my critical days for 1986. I was born on 21 June 1937.

1 Write down your age next birthday. (My age in June 1986 will be 49.)
. . . 49 . . .

2 Multiply your age by 365.
49 × 365 = 17,885

3 Add on one day for each leap year. (A leap year occurs every four years.) Don't include a leap year if February 29

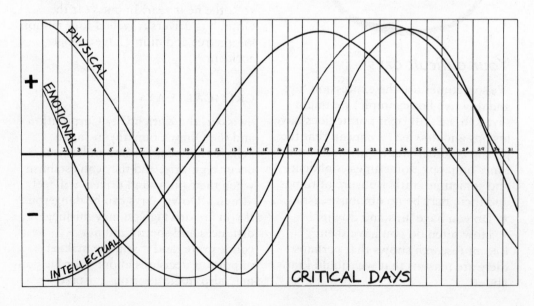

CRITICAL DAYS

is before your birth date in your birth year or after your birthday in the year you are in.
(I have lived through 12 leap years.)
17,885 + 12 = 17,897

4 Physical: Divide your total days by 23.

Take the number of remaining days (3) and count back from your next birthday. That date (18 June) will be when your physical rhythm crosses the average line and changes from a 'down' to an 'up'.

5 Intellectual: Divide your total days by 33.

Then take the number of remaining days (11) and count back from your next birthday. That date (10 June) will be when your intellectual rhythm crosses the average line and changes from a 'down' to an 'up'.

6 Emotional: Divide your total days by 28.

Then take the number of remaining days (5) and count back from your next

birthday. That date (16 June) will be when your emotional rhythm crosses the average line and changes from a 'down' to an 'up'.

7 Now you have the three critical dates nearest to your birthday. Take your diary and count backwards to find the critical days which are waiting for you! Of course, there are two critical days in each rhythm.

So you count backwards half the number of days:
physical 11.5 days
intellectual 16.5 days
emotional 14 days

8 And remember that two or (even worse) three critical days on the same date are more serious!
(During the three months before 21 June 1986 I will have one triple crossing on 21 April. Triples are particularly nasty. On 30 June I will have a double crossing.)

Reading tea leaves

What a friendly activity this can be! You've had a cup of tea (or coffee, or wine or any other drink!) and then you glance into your friend's cup and say, 'Oh! That's interesting!' And your friend is immediately fascinated! 'What can you see?' You might believe that it is possible to read your friend's future in the tea leaves (or other little bits after the coffee, wine, etc. has been drunk) at the bottom of his or her cup. I don't think it is possible really, but I

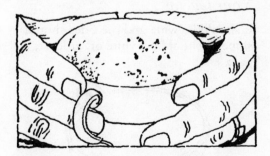

do think that your imagination can produce some wonderful ideas and if you are sensitive to your friend then, perhaps, you will be very wise.

A bit of history

A bit of history is always useful. People usually like to hear something interesting . . .

People have been drinking tea in China for thousands of years. And in China people traditionally use bells to drive away bad spirits. Chinese teacups don't have handles so they look like bells. Perhaps it was for this reason that they thought that teacups were mystical.

Lead and wax

You can use lead or wax instead of tea. You must heat up the lead or the wax and then drop the hot liquid into cold water. It will immediately cool and become an interesting shape.

Your teacup

It should be wide and the sides should slope. It should be white or, at least, pale.

The tea

A tea bag is hopeless! You need quite big leaves and you shouldn't stop them going into the cup when you pour the tea.

What you should do

When your friend has nearly finished his or her cup they should hold it in their left hand and turn it round rapidly in a clockwise direction three times. The tea should reach the top of the cup. Then your friend must turn the cup upside down and count to seven. Now you take the cup, turn it the right way up and hold it so that the handle is facing you.

Reading the leaves

Well, it will look a shapeless mess at first! You will probably feel hopeless! But just relax and look for shapes which remind you of something. It is like looking at a cloud or into a fire and seeing shapes of things you recognise. First of all, you must get a general impression. Where are the leaves? Different parts of the cup mean different things. And how are the different shapes related to each other?

Different parts of the cup

The part of the cup by the handle is your friend's home. Shapes which seem to point towards the handle are approaching, and shapes which seem to point away from the handle are departing. Shapes on the other side of the cup are far from home.

Time: the top or rim of the cup is the present and the bottom is the distant future. Shapes on the very bottom of the cup are unlucky.

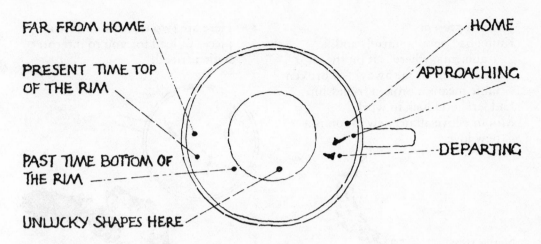

FAR FROM HOME

PRESENT TIME TOP OF THE RIM

PAST TIME BOTTOM OF THE RIM

UNLUCKY SHAPES HERE

HOME

APPROACHING

DEPARTING

Numbers

Numbers also show you time. For example, a heart and a number five could mean that your friend will have a happy experience in five days (or weeks if that is what you feel is more suitable). Numbers by themselves mean the following:

1 You will become stronger in some way.

2 You will get an opportunity to do something nice. Don't miss it this time!

3 Visiting people.

4 Good business.

5 Luck in friendship and love.

6 Good for health and work.

7 Good for partnerships.

8 An unexpected change.

9 Good for new ideas and understanding

Lines

Lines are journeys. Clear lines, wavy lines, confused lines, broken lines are what you might expect! And which shapes do the lines go near?

A FEW SHAPES

Here are a few examples of the meanings of different shapes. They will help you to read your friend's tea leaves.

Aeroplane: look for its direction and position in the cup; a sudden journey

Bird: good news

Cat: a friend who is unfair to you; a cat near the handle is good news

Dot: a dot by itself means nothing, but it makes the nearest shape very important; several dots mean money

Eye: be careful

Forked line (a line which divides): you must make a decision

Gun: trouble; don't forget, which way is it pointing?

Hat: usually it means good luck but it depends where it is; if it is in the bottom of the cup it is a competitor for you!

Insect: little problems, but they will soon be over!

Jewel: a present
Knife: bad news: quarrels and
    arguments; where is it on the cup?
    Near home or far away? – a broken
    knife means a broken friendship
Ladder: good luck in work
Moon: a love affair; new moon is a
    new love

Net: a trap
Owl: bad news
Parrot: gossip

Queen: a woman friend will help you
Rabbit: be brave!
Snake: hatred; where is it on the cup?
Triangle: point upwards means good
    luck; point downwards means
    unlucky, and the importance of any
    shapes nearby is increased
Umbrella: protection: open, you find
    protection; closed, you don't find
    protection

Volcano: very emotional
Window: open, new experiences:
    closed, you are trapped and can't get
    away
Yacht: wealth and pleasure

★★ Here are two teacups and two
pieces of lead for you to interpret
with a friend!

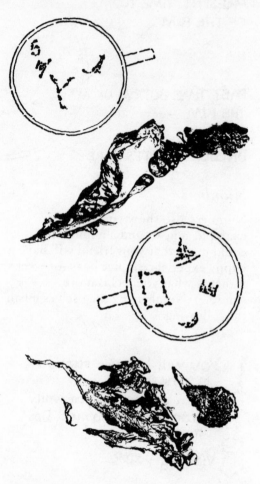

You are now ready for any situation.
You can analyse people's characters
and you can predict their difficult days
for them. And with these new skills
your own good fortune will be
guaranteed! You will be popular and
entertaining! Why not try some of the
techniques on yourself and your
friends? Remember, everyone expects
fortune tellers to be calm and confident
– you must appear to know what you
are doing!

Dowsing

Dowsing means looking for and finding water and metals, etc. by using a dowsing rod.

Dowsing really works! Dowsers are employed by industrial firms to look for pipes and cables and by civil engineers and agricultural experts who are looking for water. Expert dowsers can find underground streams and springs. People have been dowsing for thousands of years and there are dowsers in very early cave paintings.

In the past professional dowsers pretended that it was very difficult to dowse. However, today, experts believe that most people can dowse! You can try to dowse anywhere – in your home, in a garden or park, in the middle of the town or in the countryside.

WHAT DO YOU NEED?

Here are two simple dowsing rods which you can make.

A metal dowsing rod

You will need some thick wire. You could use two wire coat hangers. Cut them like this:

And then bend the pieces like this:

You could just hold the wire in your hands or you could make a handle for each wire. You will need two empty, plastic pens for the handles.

A dowsing twig

Find a twig, which should be bendy but not green. (In Britain we would use hazel, willow, beech or even privet.) Your twig must be a Y shape. It should be about one cm round and about 30 cm long. Don't take the bark off.

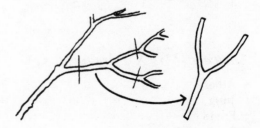

HOW TO DOWSE

A metal dowsing rod

Hold the two short ends loosely and vertically in your hands. The long pieces of the wire will be horizontal. Keep your thumbs over your forefingers. Bend your arms so that your forearms are horizontal and parallel. Keep your elbows against your body.

A dowsing twig

The palms of your hands must point upwards. And your thumbs must point outwards. Keep your elbows in to your sides and bend your arms so that your forearms and the dowsing rod are horizontal. Open the V of the twig until it is tense.

Concentrate!

Concentrate on what you want to find. Some professional dowsers carry a little sample of what they want to find in their hand between their hand and the rod. Walk slowly and continue to concentrate. Slowly cover an area of ground.

Yes!

If you find something your metal rods will cross over and your twig will turn up or down or even cross over!

A suggestion for you

Why not find a place where there is an underground stream or drain? Take your friends to a place away from the exit of the stream and see if they can find it.

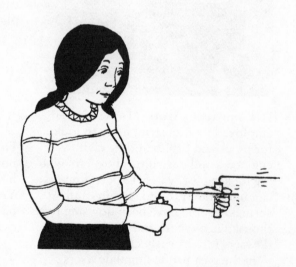

Answers (Mrs X's dream, p.51)

1 Adler
2 Jung
3 Freud

How to keep your friends happy

This section is for people who would like to know a few games. It is not for people who are responsible for organising games at parties, etc. There are plenty of books for them. I have chosen games which don't require preparation: except that you must try them out!

Games for children

Children love games, particularly simple games which they can share with an adult. And games are international; they can be played with very little language and usually need no preparation. If you can play the games which follow any child will find you very entertaining!

For little children

PEEP BO

You and one child
If they are very small they will probably love it if you hide yourself or just your face and then jump out. They will want you to do this until you are exhausted!

LOOK AT THAT

You and one child
Bend down so that your head is at their height and look at the world with them. Look at single objects and quietly describe them: 'Look at this coin.' (Trace your finger round it. Then take their finger and trace it round the edge.) 'Isn't it smooth and round? Oh, look at all those little dots on it! Can you feel them with your finger?' etc.

THIS LITTLE PIG

You and one child
You can do this with the child's hand or foot. Support the child's hand with one of yours. Take the top of the child's thumb between your thumb and forefinger and say, 'This little pig went to market.' Then take the forefinger

and say, 'And this little pig stayed at home.' Then take the next finger and say, 'This little pig ate roast beef.' Then take the next finger and say, 'And this little pig had none.' Then take the little finger and shake it for a moment, then say, 'And this little pig . . .' Run your fingers across the palm of the child's hand and up his or her sleeve and say, 'ran all the way home!'

This little pig went to market.
This little pig stayed at home.
This little pig ate roast beef.
And this little pig had none.
And this little pig ran all the way home!

THE SEA IN THE SINK

You and one child
A sink, washbowl or bowl of water
If you can get a bowl of water or, better still, go to a sink with a small child you will have a lot of fun. Tie an apron around the child. Find a good chair for the child to stand on. Make sure he or she is safe. Fill the sink or wash bowl.

Bend down so that your head is on the same level as the child's. 'It looks so shiny doesn't it . . . so sparkly. Look, the plug seems to be dancing about. You know what it looks like to me? It looks like the ocean to me . . . the great ocean crossed by sailors in their ships . . . thousands and thousands of miles, when it's calm like it is now . . . and (splash your hand in it) when it is rough!' Hopefully a few splashes will have gone on the child's face! The child may enjoy having a splash too, but don't let this go on for long! 'Shall we sail some boats?' Then find various things which will float and some that won't. You will probably spend a happy 20 minutes like this. You may need to change your clothes afterwards . . . but if you aren't used to children you will never forget the experience!

For children six to eight years old

FINGER FACES

You and one or more children
Felt tip pen
Draw faces on the ends of their fingers. Here are some for you to copy. Practise them now. You never know when you may need to do it for a child. It will give the child pleasure even if you only draw one face. If you draw more, give them different characters. Ask on which finger he or she would like to have the boy or girl . . . where they would like the king and where the bad magician, etc.

The child might like to draw some

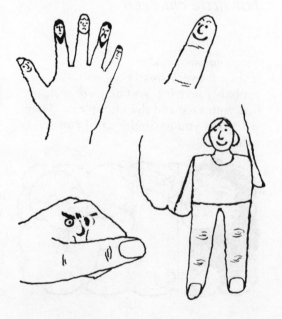

faces on your fingers. You can work out a story together. The child may have an idea immediately, if not then ask:
– What is the boy/girl called?
– What does he/she want to do?
– Why does the magician want to stop him/her doing that?
– What does the king want?
– What happens?

BLINDFOLD

You and one or more children
Scarf or handkerchief, paper and pencil
It is a strange experience to be blindfolded. Talk about what it must be like to be blind and how important all the other senses are. Here are some 'blindfold' games which will give the child the feeling of what it is like to be blind and a value of his or her other senses:
– Draw the back view of a donkey. Blindfold the child and tell him or her to draw the tail. Blindfold yourself and let the child see you try to draw the tail! (You can cut a tail out of paper and then ask the child to pin it on the donkey in the right place.)
– Describe a scene and ask the child to draw it. For example, there is a lake, and by the lake there is a little house. It has two windows and a door in the middle . . . And, once more, try to do it yourself! Children love to see a grown

up having difficulties. And they will be very kind to you about it!
– Give them something to hold and feel and to name.
– Give them something to taste and to name.

BEETLES

You and one child
Paper and pencil, and a die
If you don't have a die you will have to write the numbers one to six on six little pieces of paper.

You each try to draw a beetle. You throw the die: one for the body, two for the head, three for one eye, four for an antenna, five for a leg and six for a tail.

You must start with a one for the body. And you must have a head before you can draw the two eyes and the two antennae.

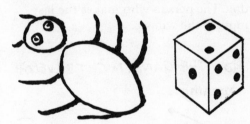

SQUARES

You and one child
Paper and pencil
Put a lot of little dots on the paper like this:

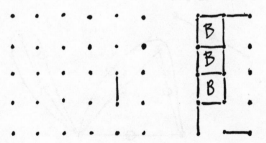

The first person joins two dots with a line. The second person joins any other two dots. And so on. The aim of the game is to put the fourth line on a square because it becomes your square and you can write your name in it.

SPROUTS

You and one child
Pencil and paper
Put six dots (this is the best number but you can draw any number) on a piece of paper anywhere. Take it in turns to draw a line which connects any two of the dots. The line can be straight or curved. It can come back to the dot from where it began and not join another dot. When you have drawn a line you must put a little circle on it.

The line must not cross over itself or any other line. The line must stop at a dot. Only three lines can come out of a dot. The person who makes the last move is the winner.

HOW THE GAME MIGHT DEVELOP

opening...

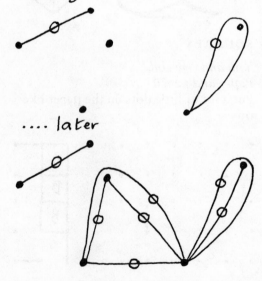

.... later

HIDE AND SEEK IN THE IMAGINATION

You and one or more children
This is a good game to play in a car. One person imagines where he or she is hiding, and the other must find out by asking questions.

You can imagine you are very small if you wish.

PAPER DOG

You and one or more children
Paper
This is how to make a dachshund and her puppies:
1 Fold a square piece of paper into four equal parts.
2 Make a letter M.
3 Fold the top corners inwards.
4 Fold the bottom corners inwards.
5 Open out the paper into an M shape.
6 Push the four top corners inside.
7 Fold back the four triangular flaps onto the body.
8 Fold each of these into half so that the points come down to make the legs.
9 Draw on the eyes and the nose.

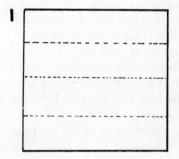

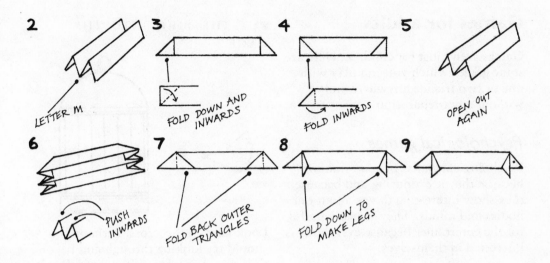

2 LETTER M

3 FOLD DOWN AND INWARDS

4 FOLD INWARDS

5 OPEN OUT AGAIN

6 PUSH INWARDS

7 FOLD BACK OUTER TRIANGLES

8 FOLD DOWN TO MAKE LEGS

9

HANGING GARDEN

You and one or more children
String

You need four pieces of string each one metre long.

1 Make two pairs. Make a cross out of the two pairs.
2 Pick the cross up.
3 Tie a knot below the cross.
4 15 cm down from the knot tie a knot in each pair.

5 Take the right-hand string from a pair and place it over the left-hand string of the next pair on the right. Tie this right-hand string to the left-hand one about 5 cm down from the main knot. Do this with each right-hand string.
6 Repeat 5 again.
7 Now tie all the strings together in one big knot.

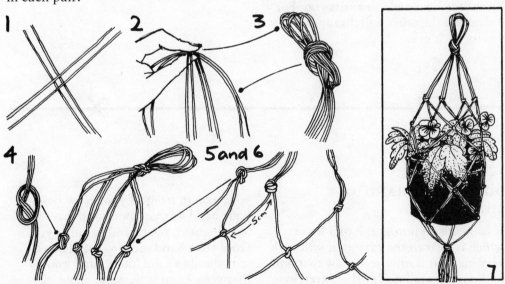

1

2

3

4

5 and 6 5cm

7

Games for adults

Games aren't just for children. Here are some games which you can play with one or two friends anywhere and without any preparation.

Psychological games

Psychological games are entertaining because they are amusing and because they show interesting things about our bodies and minds. They are very useful for the entertainer because everybody is interested in themselves.

YOUR BLIND SPOT

Did you know that you have a blind spot? Everyone has a blind spot. Here is how to 'see' yours! When you do this game for your friends you may not have this book with you! So you must be able to remember how to draw the diagram below.

Hold the diagram up in front of you about 25 cm away from your eyes. Close your left eye. Look at the square. Now move it slowly towards you. For a moment the cross will disappear. Try it with each eye.

PUT THE BIRD INTO THE CAGE

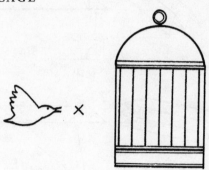

Look hard at this cross. Perhaps you should try looking through and beyond the cross. Look for quite a time. Don't move your eyes. Suddenly, you will see the bird begin to fly towards the cage and then into it! (It doesn't seem to fly into the cage for everybody.)

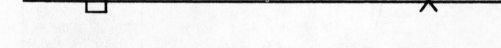

DOES YOUR HAND GET BIGGER?

If you take a photograph of a hand which is near to the camera it will look very big: if it is only 30 cm away it will look much smaller. Try this: stretch out your arm in front of you. Now bend your hand so that your palm faces you. Slowly move your hand towards you. Does your hand seem to get bigger?

It shouldn't do! Your mind knows that your hand is the same hand as

usual and that it isn't really getting bigger. So your mind translates the information and tells you that your hand is getting nearer and not bigger.

Stretch out your arm again. Bend your palm towards you. Now raise the forefinger of the other hand and place it about 20 cm from your face. Look hard at this forefinger. Concentrate on it. Now move your other hand slowly towards you and then away again.

If you concentrated on your forefinger then your other hand seemed to get bigger and then smaller again. Your mind was concentrating on your forefinger and was not able to translate the information in your eye and say that the hand was not changing size!

MEN AND WOMEN DON'T SEE THE SAME THINGS

Well, they see the same things but their minds don't interpret them in the same way! Look at the drawings below. What do they look like? Write down your idea for each one.

Research shows that men and women usually don't see the same things. According to research in Western countries most men see the first drawing as a brush or a centipede. Most women see it as a comb or teeth. Most men think the middle drawing is a target and most women think it is a dinner plate. The same number of men and women see the middle drawing as a ring or as a tyre. Most men see the right-hand drawing as a head and most women see it as a cup.

IS THE PAPER MOVING?

You will need a piece of stiff white paper or card. The card can be quite small, for example, you could use an empty cigarette packet. Fold it like this

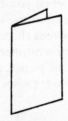

and then lay it down in front of you at chest height like this.

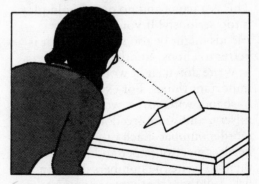

Stand or sit in front of it. Close one eye. Look at a point on the middle of the fold. Concentrate on this point for some moments. Suddenly the paper should stand up! So that it looks like this:

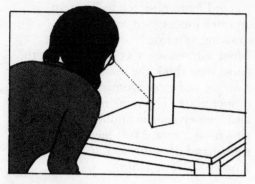

Now, slowly move your head backwards and forwards. The paper should seem to twist about!

The paper seems to stand up because your mind is not sure which point is nearer to you, the far end of the fold or the near end. Then, when you move your head, the near end of the fold moves a little more across the eye and so the mind thinks for a moment that it is nearer so it twists the paper, then it thinks it was wrong so it twists it back again!

YOUR UNCONSCIOUS SELF I

This is a game and no one should play it too seriously! If you think your friends might be too serious then it is better to choose another game.

Write down eight words naming important things. For example, husband, wife, lover, work, happiness, misery, ambition, freedom. Give each word a number. Each of your friends needs a piece of paper and pencil. Tell them to write the numbers down in a list. Tell them that you are going to say a word and they must instantly make a mark or pattern next to the first number. Tell them you will then say another word a moment later and they

must draw a mark or pattern next to the number 2, etc. Read out the words on your list quite quickly. One of your friend's pieces of paper might look like this:

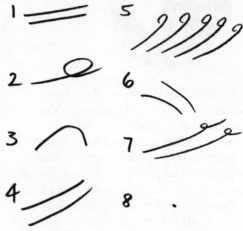

Now say the words again in order and tell them to write the words down next to each pattern.

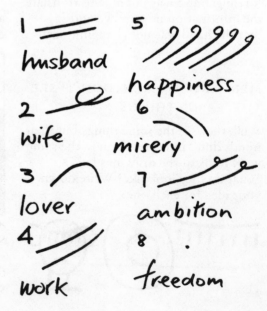

Study the marks. They will tell you what your friend feels. If any marks are similar then that means your friend has similar feelings about the words. In the example above the person thinks that work and ambition are the same. And he or she thinks that happiness is similar as well. What else does he or she think?

If all the drawings are very similar then the person is very secretive. Don't lose any friends over this game!

YOUR UNCONSCIOUS SELF 2

You need a piece of paper and a pencil. Draw this diagram on the paper. (You will need to do this for each friend.)

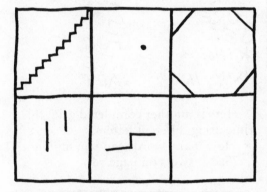

Tell your friend to draw anything at all in any or in all of the squares.
This is how you can analyse your friend's drawings:
Square 1 represents conformity (doing what everyone else does and expects).
Square 2 represents ego (self-centredness).
Square 3 represents being sociable (liking to be with others).
Square 4 represents sexual interest.
Square 5 represents interest in machines and how they work.
Square 6 represents imagination.

Here is a set of completed drawings and an analysis of them.

Square 1
The person has simply accepted that these are stairs. He or she hasn't wanted to adapt the idea or change it in any way. This shows a person who feels it is natural to conform and to do what is expected. There are other ways in which a conforming person might have drawn in this box: he or she might have simply repeated the pattern as an abstract design.

Square 2
He or she has kept the spot as the centre of his or her drawing. That shows a self-centred view of life, but needn't mean that they are selfish! It may mean that they are calm, confident and at peace with themselves.

Square 3
He or she has chosen to join the lines together. This person likes being with people.

Square 4
How many lines has he or she used to connect the two vertical lines? Only one? Then this person has only a moderate interest in sexual matters!

Square 5
The person hasn't chosen to make a

drawing of a mechanical object, so isn't mechanically minded.

Square 6

This is a very boring and well-known symbol. The person had an opportunity to do something special and didn't do it. They aren't imaginative.

★ How would you analyse this person's drawings?

Word games

PERSONAL CROSSWORDS

Each person should draw out a grid five squares by five squares. The first person calls out a letter and then everybody puts it somewhere in their grid. The players mustn't show anybody else where they are putting the letter. Players take it in turns to call out a letter.

When 25 letters have been called out and the grid is full, players count up how many words they can find and see who has the most. Diagonal words can be included. You can also include words within words, for example, 'king' is three words: 'king', 'in', 'kin'.

Here is a completed grid. I have listed the words I can find in it. Can you find any more?

A	E	O	H	K
D	T	A	N	S
B	O	R	E	F
S	E	T	G	O
P	K	I	N	G

AT   ON
OAR   DOT
BORE   GO
SET   FOG
KING   TOE
KIN IN   ART

Here is another completed grid, this time using different letters.

★ How many words can you find in it? (See answers on page 76.)

O	F	S	O	N
W	P	E	H	K
I	O	G	E	C
N	T	I	N	L
D	S	O	B	M

TEAPOT

Two people can play this game but it is better with three or four. Ask one person to move away so that the rest of you can decide on which verb you are going to choose. Let's suppose you choose 'sing'. The other person can then return; he or she must try to find out what verb you have chosen. He or she asks questions and you answer them but you never say the verb you have chosen but always use the word 'teapot', for example:

Friend: Do you teapot in the bath?
You: Yes, sometimes.
Friend: Do you teapot during meals?
You: No, not usually.
Friend: Do you enjoy teapotting?
You: Yes.
Friend: Do other people enjoy your teapotting?
You: They pretend they don't. But I'm sure they do really! etc. until your friend discovers the word.

One variation of this game is to make people laugh. The person who laughs first is the loser!

TWENTY QUESTIONS

This is a well-known game in most countries of the world. Two people can play the game but it is better with three or four. All the players except one choose an idea, usually one word (it might be the word for an object, a profession or a hobby). The other player must find out what the word is by asking questions. He or she can ask up to twenty questions. Usually the questioner is told whether the object is animal, vegetable or mineral. A good player asks very general questions to begin with rather than just guessing immediately.

Team: It's vegetable.
Questioner: Is it manufactured?
Team: Yes.
Questioner: Do people wear it?
Team: No.
Questioner: Is it found in a house?
Team: Yes. etc. until the word is found.

PASS IT ON

Another well-known game! There must be at least four people or it won't be very successful. Each player has a piece of lined paper and a pen. Everyone begins by writing the first line of a story and a few more words on the next line. Each player then folds over the paper so that the first line can't be seen and then gives it to their neighbour. The neighbour can only see the few words on the next line. He or she must continue the story, fold over the paper, making sure that there are a few words on the next line, and then pass on the piece of paper to the next neighbour. This continues until you are ready to read out the complete stories (which are usually very funny!).

He ran out of the house.
Next day he went to London
to go to the boat show.
This was his dream he grew an
enormous beard. There he stood
the childrens friend, Father
Christmas!
There was a lovely smile on
his face. Then he shouted,
The monkey got away
What a challenge. He
decided to sail away.
He would bring his dear
little friend home again.

HANGMAN

Two or more people are needed. One
person thinks of a word and draws one
short line for each letter of the word. If
the word is 'newspaper', for example,
there will be nine short lines.

The other player must then say
which letters he or she thinks might be
in the word. Any letter which is in the
word must be written on the correct
short line. If a letter is not in the word
then part of the hanged man must be
drawn. There are 13 parts to the
hanged man so only 12 wrong letters
can be guessed! The aim of the game is
to complete the word before being
hanged!

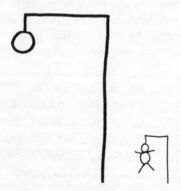

This game is obviously a good one for
concentrating on spelling. It makes the
players become more aware of which
are the common letters and which
letters often go together, for example,
'th', 'er', 'le'.

Answers (Personal crosswords)

These are the words I can find. There
may be more!

of	it
son	fee
so	feel
on	pot(s)
wind	tin
win	sob

How to be entertained

Hospitality, customs and manners

'To entertain' means to give hospitality as well as to interest and amuse. If people come to your country you will know how to look after them. You will know what kind of invitation to give them. Will you invite the visitor to your home or to a restaurant? Will you invite them to stay in your home or arrange for them to stay in a nearby hotel? Will you expect them to bring a present for you?

Ways of showing hospitality are different in every country and I have decided to concentrate on 'how to be entertained' in Britain. This section is therefore about some of the customs which you might experience if you come to Britain.

It is difficult to give any fixed rules about customs and manners in Britain. There are about 56 million people in Britain and as I am sure they all have their own ideas on these matters, I have tried to concentrate on customs and manners which are very common.

★ When you have read this section perhaps you could try to write some similar information for British people about being a visitor in your country. Would you need different sections of information? Could you use the headings I have used and substitute the information for your country? If you have similar customs and expectations in your country,
say so. Warn the British visitor of clear differences.

★★ Show your information to a friend. You may find that you don't always agree on what is generally true in your country!

Invitations

People might invite you to their home or to go out with them for the evening. They might invite you when they see you or by telephone. However, it is still quite common to be invited by letter or by invitation card. The invitation will tell you what the occasion is, when it is and, occasionally, what you should wear! Here are some examples:

Mr and Mrs Robin Hall,

Mr and Mrs John Steele
at home
Monday, July 1st

Cocktails
6.30—8.30

R.S.V.P.
Brook Cottage
Beaulieu
Hampshire

Richard and Laura Ross at home
on Friday, 21 June

CHEESE AND WINE SUPPER

R.S.V.P. 7.45 p.m.
3 Dover Road
Tunbridge Wells Tel. 3154
Kent

RSVP means, 'répondez s'il vous plaît', 'reply if you please'! This use of French is a reminder of the influence the French have had on social customs in Europe.

Mr and Mrs Cliff Williamson
request the pleasure of the company of

Miss Katy Biggs

at the marriage of their daughter

Amanda Rachel
to
Christopher Bradley

at St. John's Church, Bath Street, Chesterfield,
on Saturday 5th June at 2.00 p.m.
and afterwards at The Peacock Inn, Rowsley.

R.S.V.P. *7 Lion's Bank, Chesterfield, Derbyshire*

REPLYING TO INVITATIONS

Reply quickly. If the occasion is small then you can reply by telephone, but if it is a big occasion it is better to reply by letter. It is kinder to do this because it helps your host to remember and to organise things. If the invitation was by formal invitation then you might like to reply in a formal way. Here are two replies to the invitations above; in one reply the invitation is accepted and in the other it is not.

> 9 Birch Avenue,
> Manchester,
> M20 0BH.
>
> 10th May.
>
> Miss Katy Biggs thanks Mr and Mrs Williamson for their kind invitation to the wedding of their daughter Amanda on the 5th June and has great pleasure in accepting.

5 Park Avenue
Beaulieu
Hampshire

Mr and Mrs Hall thank Mr and Mrs Steele for the invitation to their home on July 1st, but regret they are unable to accept because of a previous engagement.

INVITATIONS TO PEOPLE'S HOMES

In Britain it is common to be invited to someone's home rather than to a restaurant. If you are invited to a restaurant it is because your host is very busy, can't cook very well, or wants to give you the enjoyment of some special type of food, or perhaps, has often invited you home and now wants to give you a special treat!

Business visitors from other countries are often invited to their British colleagues' home. However, sometimes it may be more convenient to invite a business colleague to a restaurant.

Presents

If you are invited to someone's home to have a meal it is usual to take some flowers or a box of chocolates. It is not usual to take a bottle of wine unless you know your host well. Although flowers and chocolates are quite acceptable it would be very nice if you could take something from your country.

It is different if you are invited to a party, and it also depends on what kind of party it is. Many parties these days are 'bring a bottle' parties. Unless your host is very rich then a bottle of wine is always welcome if it is a big party of say 30 or more people. Ask whether or not you should bring a bottle when you are invited if you aren't sure. Say something like, 'Can I bring a bottle?' And your host will tell you what to do.

Host: We're having a party on Saturday. I wonder if you would like to come. I'd be very pleased if you could.

You: Oh, thank you. Yes, I would love to come. What time?

Host: Well, any time really. I think most people will be coming about 8.30 to 9 o'clock.

You: How many will be coming?

Host: I imagine about forty.

You: I'll bring a bottle then.

Host: Well, that would be nice. / Oh, don't bother. I'll have plenty in the house.

Of course, if it is a formal drinks/cocktail party you wouldn't take a bottle with you.

If you are going to stay in someone's house you might like to take something from your country.

Dress

If you aren't sure what you should wear then ask your host or your friends. Usually dress is informal and individual in Britain for parties and for invitations to dinner in people's homes. If you are going to an expensive restaurant the men may have to wear a

jacket and tie, jeans wouldn't be
allowed.

Introductions

In Britain (if we remember!) we
introduce:
– men to women;
– younger people to older people.
Sometimes there might be exceptions to
these basic customs. For example, it is
sometimes difficult if the woman is
clearly very young and the man is
elderly and very senior in his work and
achievements. If a distinguished male
poet has just given a lecture then we
might introduce a young woman to
him, rather than the other way round.

You will find that many people in
Britain now introduce people by their
first names or the first and surname
together. Sometimes, on formal
occasions we introduce people by their
title, Mr, Mrs, Miss, etc. Customs
change and all you can do is to listen
and look and see what the people
around you are doing.

John Race: Mr Hawkins. May I
introduce Miss Williams to you?
Miss Williams. Mr Hawkins. (They
shake hands.)
Mr Hawkins: How do you do? I'm very
pleased to meet you.

Miss Williams: Hello. I'm so glad to
meet you. I love your poetry.
John Race: Miss Williams, I'd like to
introduce Brian Parker to you.
Brian, this is Miss Williams.
Miss Williams: Hello, nice to meet you.
Brian Parker: Hello.
John Race: Mr Hawkins, I believe you
know Mr Parker don't you?
Mr Hawkins: Yes, of course. Hi, Brian.
How are things?

INTRODUCING YOURSELF

If you are at a party you can go up to
another person and introduce yourself.
'Hello, my name is Andrew Vincent.
Are you a friend of . . .?' You don't
have to wait to be introduced. And, by
the way, at parties we assume that
everyone will talk to a lot of people. It
is quite normal for someone to have a
short conversation with you and then
go on to talk to other people! Don't
think they dislike you or that they are
impolite! It is the custom at many
parties in Britain, particularly where
people are standing up rather than
sitting down.

Here are two ways of finishing a conversation at a party: 'Excuse me. I think I'll go and get another drink. See you later, perhaps?' 'Oh, excuse me. I've just seen Mary Jennings over there. I've got to discuss a meeting we are having on Thursday. Would you excuse me for a moment?'

SHAKING HANDS

In Britain we often shake hands when we meet someone for the first time or meet after a long absence. And we shake hands on leaving each other if we are not going to see each other again or for a long time. We don't shake hands every time we meet as is the custom in some countries.

Punctuality

If you are invited to dinner at someone's home you shouldn't arrive earlier than the time given and you shouldn't arrive more than about 15 minutes late. If you are going to be late telephone and let your host know so that the meal can be delayed.

Dinner is usually served between 8pm and 9pm. Very often guests are invited to arrive earlier than this so that they can have a drink and be introduced to the other guests.

HOW LONG SHOULD YOU STAY?

Watch other guests! But if you are the only guest leave before midnight if it is a weekday evening and if you or your host must work the next day.

If the conversation is really full of life at midnight and you would like to stay longer say, 'What time do you usually go to bed?' And then your host

can say whether they would like to finish the evening.

Bigger parties are usually held at weekends and often go on until 2am or even later.

Pubs

Pubs are popular places in Britain. People can meet each other in an informal atmosphere. They don't have to be too polite! Nevertheless there are one or two customs you should know. If you have been invited to the pub then your friend will buy your first drink. If you want to go on drinking then he or she will probably expect you to buy the next 'round' of drinks! It is very common for a group of people to take it in turns to buy all the drinks and that can be quite expensive. If that is the custom your friends are following then, unfortunately, you must follow it too! If you really have just arrived from another country they may excuse you. You can buy non-alcoholic drinks in a pub . . . but you are still expected to pay your round.

Women are as welcome in most pubs as men and in many pubs it is quite normal for two or more women to enjoy an evening without men. There is no reason why a woman should not pay for and order a round of drinks.

Last thoughts

We can't all be entertaining in the same way. Some of us are naturally quiet and some are happy to dominate a room full of people. The main secret of being a successful entertainer is to be sensitive to other people, to their interests and feelings. And this applies to a room full of people or to a single companion. Interest, fun, drama and challenge all lie within each one of us. The successful entertainer doesn't put them there but releases them. I hope this book has entertained you. And I hope that you, in turn, will be able to use some of the ideas to entertain others.

Acknowledgements

The author and publishers are grateful
to the following, who have given
permission for the use of copyright
material identified in the text.

Robin Blythe-Lord for the photograph
on p. xii; The Supreme Magic
Company Ltd for the advertisement on
pp. 13–14; Barry Jones for the
photographs on p. 15; Bill Godfrey for
the photographs on pp. 21, 63.